With love to Stevie and Jack,  ⌐erleaders.

With gratitude for God, Buddha, Universe and my Monks who guide me and keep me on my path.

Just Give Your Head a Shake...

and Change Your Life for the Better

By: Cheryl Hitchcock

iUniverse, Inc.
New York   Bloomington

Just Give Your Head a Shake
and Change Your Life for the Better

iUniverse books may be ordered through booksellers or by contacting:

iUniverse
1663 Liberty Drive
Bloomington, IN 47403
www.iuniverse.com
1-800-Authors (1-800-288-4677)

Because of the dynamic nature of the Internet, any Web addresses or links contained in this book may have changed since publication and may no longer be valid.

ISBN: 978-1-4401-7984-6 (sc)
ISBN: 978-1-4401-7985-3 (dj)
ISBN: 978-1-4401-7986-0 (ebk)

Library of Congress Control Number: 2009910411

Printed in the United States of America

iUniverse rev. date: 12/2/2009

Contents

ABOUT THE AUTHOR

My wish for every person who reads this book is to elevate your quality of life in some way. For the past 13 years, this is what I have been doing professionally with my clients. The journey has been amazing and somewhat strange at  times, but always an educational experience. And isn't that what life is about? A chance to learn and grow and become the best person you can, all the while living an abundant life full of purpose and wonderment.

It's funny how things in life turn out. I started my life living at the same home I now live in; the only difference is that I own it now. I grew up in Toronto, Ontario, Canada. From there I moved around to various locations in Ontario, just to end up back in the very place from which I started.

One of the moves I made was to Barrie Ontario where I went to College to gain my Diplomas in Developmental Disabilities and Addictions. I accepted internships at Penetanguishene's Hospital where I worked with people who were diagnosed with a Dual Diagnosis (Developmental Disabilities and Mental Illness), as well as clients from Oakridge Penitentiary. I also interned at Barrie and District's Association for People with Special Needs and the Barrie Catholic School Board, and in Toronto at the Donwood Institute and the Centre for Addiction and Mental Health's Problem Gambling Program.

While still living in Barrie, I felt that Toronto kept calling me back, and through a series of events and obligations I ended up back in Toronto and went to work for the Addiction Research Foundations Withdrawal Management Unit. From there I pursued an opportunity to work for the University Health Networks Withdrawal Management Unit and then moved to the Canadian Mental Health Association where I was a Concurrent Disorders Specialist on an Assertive Community Treatment team, working in the community with people who had severe and persistent psychotic illnesses. I obtained my Forensic Certification in High Risk Sexual Deviance and Anger Management, through the collaboration of the Centre for Addiction and Mental Health and the University of Toronto, thus enabling me to work with people who were deemed NCR (Not Criminally Responsible) through mental disease or defect (formerly known as the criminally insane).

Throughout my career, I had done counselling with mainstream individuals who did not posses any psychiatric diagnosis but were stressed individuals trying to manage their busy lives. I found that the counselling methods that I was using with my psychiatric clients worked well for my mainstream clients with just a bit of tweaking (I didn't have to manage the psychosis or cognitive impairments). But stress is stress and it can have devastating and lasting effects on our minds and bodies.

A few years ago, I felt the Universe tugging very strongly at me to leave the agency I had been working for and venture out on my own. Luckily for me I had learned a few things along the way, not the least of which is how to manage stress. I also learned how to use my energy to direct me and to manifest what I need, and it works like a charm. The spiritual side of my work was provided to me by Buddhist Monks, Physicists (yes physicists) and Shaman who taught me not only how to meditate but also how to expand my mind to bring about alignment with the Universal Laws and the energy that resonates with and through all of us and everything else in our world.

I was guided to bring this information and help forward to the masses and have endeavoured daily to do just that. It is with that message that I felt compelled to write this book and what I am sure will be a series of books that outline therapeutic issues as well as spiritual guidance. I have always felt that these two aspects work hand in hand and when combined they will bring about not only an elevated quality of life but also an abundant and awe inspiring existence, encompassing all that we as divine spirits can envision for ourselves. My hope is that you will enjoy this book as much as I've enjoyed bringing it to you. Remember to always pass on your positive experiences to others; it will have a wonderful impact on all of us.

You can contact Cheryl at
www.integritycounsellingservices.com or
416-919-9831
1-877-919-9831

INTRODUCTION

When writing this book I had to take stock of my life's path; what I am here to accomplish, what is meaningful to the clients that I work with and what outcome I hope to achieve.

The purpose of this book is to give you, my readers, the knowledge and tools that I have acquired from working with my clients. I hope you can use the information in this book to enhance your own lives. It serves no higher purpose in my life to keep the valuable knowledge I have obtained to myself. I would much rather share what I know with my clients; both current and future. I do not operate with a sense of competition when it comes to helping people. Of course without my clients, I would have no business. However; my ultimate goal as a therapist and coach is to help them achieve success.

I also would like to stress that for the purpose of this book, I will not reference any particular religious group and will instead use the term Universal Energy Source to define not only our individual and collective energy but to speak to the higher power, God Source, Intuitive or Subconscious mind. If you prefer to refer to your higher source as God, Buddha, Allah, Jehovah, Mother Earth or another reference then please feel free to substitute your own word for Universal Source. It is about your higher connection and not about the label. It is the internal omnipresent yet intangible power that we tap into from time to time that we express as miracles or unexplainable phenomena.

Through a series of what I refer to as major life events, I came to be where I am today; a woman with clear vision, and exemplary direction. I now know exactly what my purpose is and the path that I am meant to follow. My formal and spiritual guidance and education was granted to me by the Universe at a time when I could recognize, understand and use it to better my own life. As a result, I align myself with the Universe to help change the lives of others.

While I was practicing under the guidance of Monks, I learned how to connect with my Inner Source through meditation practices. I gained knowledge and deep introspection through Buddhist teachings and philosophies. The Monks taught me how to expand my mind and harness my internal energy in order to produce profound and fundamental changes in my life; changes that I teach others to do for themselves. Since that time, I have endeavoured to experience all that the great healers and sages have to teach me. I have had the great honour to learn from, and observe some very powerful Shaman, Monks, healers, physicists and sages; all of whom have helped guide my knowledge and education to an absolutely amazing phenomena experience.

Until a decade or so ago, I had not yet fully discovered my life path. In reflecting on my life, I knew that at a young age I was aware of certain things about myself that lead me to the path that I am on now. I often felt like I was stumbling along and falling, unsuspecting, into the proper direction. I felt like I was being knocked around in life, yet I somehow always managed to land on my feet, only to be guided in a different direction over and over again. The more negative a situation was for me, the better off I would land. Life sometimes doesn't make sense and I believe we simply shouldn't waste our time wondering why this is.

While I was guided by this strong internal drive to keep striving for more, I always intuitively knew that I was meant to do something profound with my life. I am so grateful for my drive to explore, in spite of the criticism and negative energy I received. As a result, I learned to keep most of my thoughts to myself. I gained no clear direction or perceptive advice from my family and continued the 'stumble of life' to find my path. My spiritual teachings have taught me that everything happens for a reason, I am therefore able to understand my past more clearly. If you open yourself to receive, the Universe will provide you with all that you need. I am a perfect example of this.

I knew by the time I was a teenager that I had an innate ability to analyze human behaviour. I could tell when people were not being 'real' in spite of how they projected themselves to the world. But I didn't know what to do with it, until I opened my mind to receive direction from the Universe. I wasn't quite clear what my path would look like or how it would come about, but I followed my intuition and I am grateful that I did. I ended up squarely on my perfect path and I am able to grow spiritually. Every day I continue to experience an awe and amazement that only the Universal Source can provide.

My formal education did not simply consist of psychology or social work, although it certainly contains a mix of both. My education revolves around abnormal psychology, mental health, behaviour modification, nursing, counselling and developmental disabilities. In addition to my diploma, I hold a post graduate diploma in the addictions field. My years of study basically revolve around whatever could go wrong with a human being. My education is another example of my intuitive ability to focus on my future life path. I didn't understand at the time why I was enrolled in my studies; but what I was studying at the time just seemed to fit.

It was not until after I had been working in a clinical setting that I discovered my need for spiritual connection. Quite literally, one day I found myself knocking on the door of a Buddhist Temple wondering if I should run away before someone actually answered. I decided to stay and face what was on the other side of the door. After all, weren't Buddhists supposed to be kind? Regardless, I decided that the 'school of hard knocks' I grew up in was excellent preparation for any type of rejection I may face. Luckily however, rejection was not an option. The door opened and I was ushered in; beginning my life changing experience. I finally found a place where I was accepted wholly and unconditionally. I had a desire to learn about higher consciousness and spirituality and they were in a unique position to teach me. I spent years at this Buddhist Temple working with the Monks and fine tuning my spiritual skills. But like life, spiritual pursuits are never fully learned.

This experience, as with other experiences in my life, significantly helped improve myself as a person and my life as a whole. I compare this time to coming across a magic wand that has worked to make my dreams come true. My life and my path became clearer and focused after this experience. I realized I could harness the power of my mind to bring about a wonderful existence for myself. I was so awestruck by this that I had to spread the word. Unfortunately, the world was not ready to hear it.

After many years of providing clinical counselling and working with marginalized populations, I began to learn how to incorporate my spiritual and formal education into my therapy sessions. I found that when I integrated therapeutic with spiritual strategies, my clients were better able to manage their problems and their quality of life drastically improved. Some clients were able to pursue dreams they never thought possible before. So of course I continued this practice.

Unfortunately, just as the world at large was not ready to hear about my spiritual understanding and skills, neither was the agency I worked for. I felt restricted by the mandate of care that my agency was funded for and at odds with my place there and how to work with both of my passions, counselling and spirituality. With a leap of faith and guidance from the Universe, I decided to go out on my own and start my counselling practice. I continue to work with my clients from a counselling perspective but also incorporate a large spiritual component. I'm proud to say it's working like a charm.

I now feel compelled to help all of you find your own Universal Source as well as provide information that will help you overcome negative behaviours and stress so you too can live a consciously manifested life.

When I first discovered what I could do and bring into my life by using the power of my mind and the Universal Energy Source, I was absolutely astonished! I was in pure awe by the power that resonated not only within me, but all around me. I knew that I had to share this knowledge with others. My desire to enlighten was overwhelming. This experience changed my life completely and I knew it would change other peoples. As I worked with my clients and taught them how to harness their own energy and mind power to bring about profound change, I began to see amazing results with them. It was like night and day. The positive effects spread like wildfire.

This is not just a spiritual book. This book is also a compilation of clinical counselling practices. The counselling aspect of my life is that of science and psychology. I have incorporated this into my therapy sessions. I have been open minded and trusting throughout my life but I have also been cynical, always requiring evidence before believing that something will work. I strongly believe in seeing the outcome firsthand before believing what someone else says. I use this philosophy when working with my own clients. I urge them to go out in the world and apply the strategies I suggest to change their lives and I will ask you, the readers, to do the same.

The analytical part of me is grateful for the scientific evidence available demonstrating the power of the mind, including our own energy to change any aspect of our life; our health, genetics and disease. I personally don't think that we need to scientifically prove spirituality in order to utilize it. We certainly do not require this evidence with organized religion. Scientific evidence is something that we, as critical Westerners, have come to rely on for credibility.

This book discusses some of the most popular issues that my clients present to me. They are also issues that have been the most life changing for them. I had to write about perceptions and beliefs in order to give some foundation to the underlying challenges that we face every day.

This book was created to help people overcome their personal problems and challenges. If I can educate you how to fix things when they go awry, then we all benefit. My hope is that this book will help you overcome the 'stuff that keeps you stuck' and benefit from all that the Universe has to offer. I will not only provide you with educational facts to help you understand the information you are reading, but I will also provide you with some tried and true strategies and tools that you can implement if you so choose. Once you have put these strategies into use, you will most certainly undergo significant change in your life.

For all of you who read this book, my wish is to help you benefit from my 'roundabout' path and to seek a straighter, clearer path for yourselves. My perspective is coming from a place of higher elevation and quality of life. So open your mind and see for yourself. Enjoy!

CHAPTER 1

THOUGHTS, PERCEPTIONS & BELIEFS

(How they're formed)

We all start off in life as perfect human beings. We are born with no judgements, criticisms or negativity. We begin as tiny beings with an amazing ability to meet our own basic needs. Babies are, without effort, able to be one with the world and the essence of our energy. They don't rationalize if something is good or bad; they just know. These amazing spiritual beings can't walk or talk but they have the ability to position themselves as our top priority and make no excuses for their demands. They seem to live in accordance with the universe with little or no effort.

Then we (their parents and caregivers) step in and impose our views, opinions, reservations, beliefs, etc. on these tiny beings; shaping the beginning of a lifelong belief system. Although babies have thoughts, they don't put any conditions on their thoughts until they are taught by others in their environments to do so. Infants don't look at their parents and judge them. They just know that these people will meet their needs for nourishment, as well as their other basic needs for survival. They are fearless until they are told (or find out for themselves) that something is harmful to them. Babies don't look at you and think that you're too fat or your hair is frizzy! Thank goodness children learn to walk and talk and become toilet trained before they are filled with fears and negative perceptions, or they would still be learning into adulthood!

We gain our perceptions from the world around us and the people in it. Poor, naive, scared (or strong, excited, knowledgeable) first-time parents are bombarded with information about how to raise their children even before the day they are born. How many times do we hear that the way a woman's stomach carries the baby – high or low – determines the sex? Or that if you listen to the wrong type of music while pregnant your children will be hyperactive criminals! These 'theories' are ridiculous, but do people believe them? Yes they do! People believe things based on the beliefs and perceptions they have adopted, and that have been handed down to them over the course of their lives.

It is within our brain that our beliefs and perceptions are born. Your brain is the hard-drive of your body as well as your mind. Your brain takes in all information, whether it is verbal, non-verbal, or sensory. It has the ability to determine whether or not something is pleasant, right or wrong and holds no foundation for context. The labels that we assign to anything and everything are what determine how we view them. Babies and toddlers don't know what anything is until we teach them what the label is. A carrot is called a carrot because that is what someone once decided to name it. The actual carrot does not know that it is a carrot, it just grows.

I'm not knocking labels; labels are necessary to help us easily and consistently navigate through life. We need rules, laws and civilization to keep us safe and to prevent chaos, (although I suppose you could argue that the world seems to already be in chaos) but that's just an observation, isn't it? We choose how we view our world based on our own perceptions and beliefs. If a person is prone to adopt a negative perception of the world, he or she will be more likely than others to perceive the world as being in chaos. If a person adopts a more positive view of the world, he or she would more likely perceive the world as being an overall peaceful and wonderful place. Technology allows us to gain a firsthand glimpse into the many wars being waged across the world. Whether or not these wars have an impact on our lives is based on our individual mindsets.

I cannot help but find it perplexing that many of the wars being waged are based on religious beliefs. My perception of religion is that they all are based on being 'good' people and doing 'good' things, so I find it to be such a paradox when people fight for their perception of being 'good' and doing 'good'. I realize that this observation may seem grossly simplistic to some but we must go back to our basic foundation of personal belief and views to understand just how ridiculous some things appear. Our thoughts are what drives our actions, but they are often based on long-standing beliefs and perceptions that you may not have had at all unless they were handed down to you by those in your earliest environments.

Luckily, we can and do have the ability to change our thoughts, belief systems and insights. It turns out that

3

it is possible to 'teach an old dog new tricks'! We have often heard statements like, "I'm too old to change my ways". Well I am here to tell you that you are never too old to change! Anything you learn, you can unlearn and relearn, and this is what I help people understand and do in my counselling practice. It begins with our own understanding of how perceptions and beliefs are formed. After all, we would be calling a carrot an orange today if that is what it had been named.

Have you ever been to a party with a friend and discussed the event with one another at the end of the night? Your friend may gush about what a great party it was; the music was fantastic and the food was amazing. And you may strongly disagree. You may feel as though the people at the party were boring, the music was awful and the food lacked taste. Your observation of the night may be so different that anyone would wonder if you two were at the same party! Individual perceptions are based on strong lifelong beliefs. Our belief systems cause judgements and our perceptions are based on our individual view of the world and everything in it.

Our beliefs can impact our abstract reasoning and how we view concepts. We have different hemispheres in our brains that are responsible for our ability to learn concepts and abstract reasoning, but it is our beliefs and perceptions that shape them, and give us context. We have to be willing to open our minds to change, and believe in our own ability to modify our lives. It will come down to what you choose to do that will determine how, and what you change about yourself or your life. Like I mentioned before, anything you learn can be unlearned and relearned. Everything in life is a learning experience. You decide what to learn, unlearn or relearn based on the awareness you have of yourself and your abilities.

You then make your own choice to go ahead or not go ahead with change.

As humans, we make approximately 20,000 choices per day. Thankfully, most of our decisions are made subconsciously. Otherwise we would be pretty mentally exhausted!

Your everyday choices are based on your beliefs and perceptions sometimes without you even being consciously aware. Think about what it would be like to consciously think about what direction you are going to take to cross the floor from the coffee bar to the elevator at your workplace. Or if you had to think about every turn you are taking during the day, and if that is the turn you should make? You make your everyday decisions based on your own opinion. Because of these internal feelings, you are able to subconsciously know the fastest way to get from point A to point B. I'm confident that you can attest that these perceptions and beliefs have proven effective to you over time.

Isn't a good thing we don't have to consciously make every decision throughout the day? If we had, we would get nothing accomplished and be completely overwhelmed.

I urge you to give some of your mental energy to this topic so you can gain a clearer understanding of what makes us all individuals, and so you can embrace our differing beliefs and perceptions. It will help all of us to have a more open, objective and hopefully inclusive mindset regarding our fellow human beings. Being tolerant and accepting of one another will not only benefit our own selves, but the world. After all, we are all interconnected on this planet and the Universe.

Cheryl Hitchcock

Understanding one another's concepts of perceptions, thoughts and beliefs will help us to diminish our judgements of each other and will result in greater harmony. These outcomes will surely only benefit us as humans coexisting on this planet. As long as something does not create harm for people why not give it a try, or at least a thought?

CHAPTER 2

CHANGING YOUR PERCEPTIONS

In Chapter 1 we looked at how thoughts, perceptions and beliefs are formed. My experience has taught me that it is easier for people to change what they see as negative if they know where it comes from. It's not enough to just engage in a new behaviour without having a true understanding of how the behaviour manifested itself in the first place. I call this superficial change a "band-aid" solution. I like to get to the underlying reasons why behaviour manifests and persists. I think it is prudent for the purpose of this book to understand that when I use the word 'behaviours' that technically a behaviour is anything we say, think, or do.

I do use band-aid solutions in acute situations with my clients to overcome immediate behaviours that are proving harmful to them in some way. For example, if I have a client who is experiencing devastating anxiety or panic attacks, and theses attacks are preventing the client from physically doing what they need to do, I will engage in short term strategies to help them overcome the immediate or acute anxiety-related behaviours. In this way, the client will be able to move towards a healthier, more functional life in the present. I will then start to explore, at a deeper level, how the anxiety manifested itself, and how the client can overcome it for the long term. This is where the counselling aspect comes into play. I will talk more about stress and anxiety in Chapter 5.

Our perceptions and beliefs for the most part are ingrained, and our thoughts and patterns of behaviour are dictated by these feelings. If your perceptions and beliefs have been a part of you for a long time, you might think to change them is too difficult. It is not. It may not happen overnight, as any significant change requires work, but I assure you that you will extract an unbelievable sense of self pride and a drive to do and be more when you succeed.

Anything you learn requires effort and consistency. Many people give up easily when they attempt a new way of being or doing something and it does not work out right away. It serves to reinforce the adage that "you can't teach an old dog new tricks". Well, I'll say this again; it's a good thing some of our most significant behaviours, like walking, talking and becoming toilet trained, were learned before the age of three! Otherwise, those with negative attitudes towards change would be in a mess of trouble. You absolutely can teach an old dog new tricks, and you can change long standing negative behaviours, beliefs and perceptions. You just need an open mind and a willingness to transform your life.

Take smoking for example, it is one of the toughest addictions to overcome; to some this habit can be even more addictive than heroin. Before I work on any addiction or significant change in a client's life, I will let them know hard work is required on their part. But in the end, the client will only have themselves to thank. Even though I provide them the tools to help them on their path, they have to do the work alone; therefore the gratitude and congratulations will be theirs to bask in. They may stumble and fall throughout their journey and that's where I come in, to give them a hand up and provide them with more focus. My job is to instil hope, educate the client about their issue, dig deeper in the basis of their issue, and give them tools to help in their efforts to change. Anyone can change behaviour for the short term, but it's the long term, life sustaining change that we are after here. It is therefore imperative to recognize and understand how the issue first came about and how it evolved from there.

With addictions, the general rule of thumb is that you can expect it to take half the life of the addiction for it to cease being a problem. This book doesn't include a whole chapter on addictions, but I will point out that, in Canada, we are taught to believe that an addiction is not inherently a disease. We practice harm and risk reduction, moderation and controlled use, as well as abstinence. We do not focus solely on the medical model to understand addiction issues. Because people can and are able to drink alcohol in a social and recreational way, for example, someone who has been labelled an alcoholic will not be treated as though he or she has a disease. No one theory covers all factors making up an addiction so we therefore choose not to label addictions solely as a disease. This is more about opinions and treatment issues. This is a great example of differing perceptions and beliefs. Whatever the client holds as his or her particular perception or belief about addictions, I will work with, and move forward from there.

If you can change a perception or belief about a particular issue, especially one that is proving to be detrimental to you, then you can make lifelong changes that will be positive and successful. It is difficult to see our way out of a negative situation when we only have one view and opinion about that issue. We tend to start going in circles, trying the same things and expecting different results. And we know that change doesn't work that way. We need to expand our minds and change thoughts. New results will follow when we open our minds to allow new ways of thinking to come in.

Many people choose to believe that they do not have control over what happens in their lives and have chosen to surrender to or settle for whatever 'junk' comes their way. Others may judge them as spineless, cowards, losers or door mats. It generally is not that way with these folks. It is our perception and belief that they are okay with the junk, whether it is people whom they choose to have relationships with, their employers, colleagues, or even situations that crop up in their own lives. Others may judge them as "easy going" or "lasse faire", or of not caring what happens to them. This is generally not the way with these folks. Of all of the people that I have spoken with over the years who fall into this category, most of them would like to live somewhere in the middle. They do care about how they are treated; they want more respect and they want to be taken more seriously for their viewpoints. Usually what happens is that they don't know how to change and when they have made attempts, someone significant in their lives shoots them down, and they feel foolish, hurt or frustrated. So they go back to what is normal for them and adjust their perceptions and beliefs accordingly, so that they can feel comfortable again. This may be dysfunctional, but it is what is normal for that person.

It doesn't have to be this way. We can and do dictate how others treat us. Yes, this does apply to the negative treatment as well. You may say that you don't want to be treated disrespectfully, but then you must look at what you allow into your life. Often times people will be treated with disrespect in public, but are reluctant to stand up for themselves, or stand their ground on an issue for fear of looking more foolish, or starting a 'scene'. This does not have to happen. When someone speaks to you in a fashion that does not honour you as a person, you need to have the courage to speak up. This does not have to be done in an argumentative way; in fact, it should be done in an assertive and factual manner and with a conversational tone. This allows you to state your expectations and also allows the other person to get the message and leave the conversation with his or her dignity intact. It is not in anyone's best interest nor does it honour our spirit to "win" the fight by knocking the other person down. You will end up with more respect from others as well as the person who disrespected you.

For example, if someone says to you, "You failed, are you stupid"? You just look at them and say (in an even but assertive tone) "Please don't speak to me like that again". You don't need to defend yourself or justify your position. The person with whom you are speaking will get the message. If they don't seem to get it then just maintain your statement and refuse to engage with their behaviour. You want to send the message that it is not okay for people to speak to you in a disrespectful manner, and you will also convey that the statement they made is not acceptable. In no way does this make you look foolish, but it does send a clear message as to how you would like to be treated. Use this strategy for any situation you feel disrespected. I would recommend that after stating your position three times, and that person continues to speak to you disrespectfully, you leave the location or refuse to engage further.

You can also state how you feel and what you would like to see changed by using the following formula: "I feel (insert an emotion) when you (insert the offending behaviour), and I would like (insert behaviour you would like to see). So for example, "I feel <u>frustrated</u> when you <u>interrupt me when I'm speaking</u> and I would like <u>you to listen to what I have to say before you reply</u>". This statement will first of all let the person know how you are feeling without attacking him or her, as well as how you would like to be treated. It is clear and gives the other person a concrete way of treating you in the future.

You need to be assertive in your statements and you must take it upon yourself to change the way you wish to be treated, without making the other person feel attacked or foolish. You need to give the other person a way out of the situation with their dignity intact, or they may become defensive or angry, sparking more disrespectful behaviour. It also may help the other person realize a disrespectful behaviour they may not have been aware of previously.

Some people will want to engage your ego and persist in negative and destructive communication patterns. Stick to your position, and others will quickly realize that you are not willing to engage the ego, and will treat you the way that you want. This is their issue to realize and not your problem to overcome. Don't lose your cool with disrespectful people. These people, after all, are operating from their perceptions and belief systems that are different from yours. They have learned these behaviours, and like yourself, should be given the same opportunities to increase their awareness and pursue their own change, if they so choose. Try to tap into your spiritual being when dealing with those who would like to treat you with disrespect. Remember that you are a divine spiritual being and you deserve to be treated with respect. You will also become increasingly aware of how you treat others in your interactions with them. The goal is always to try to create a 'win-win' situation, so that all people are treated with respect and are honoured simply because they exist. Your spiritual self is not ego based and does not care to win in any situation, but to create more situations for spiritual contact.

Remember that everyone has their own individual perceptions and beliefs. You can only work on yourself; you cannot expect anyone else to change their feelings and opinions. So don't get frustrated! When the people close to you, who care about you, see the change that you are undertaking, it may spark their own change. After all, the modifications you are making are positive ones. Those people in your life will take note of your transformation and may ask what you are doing.

This brings me to a particularly odd set of behaviours that you may see crop up when you're on your path to positive change. The behaviours may not be your own, but those of people who are close to you or have an impact on your life. I'm talking about the saboteurs. Saboteurs are people who do not feel comfortable with your change and may experience fear around your change. Often times, saboteurs are people who are closest to you. They fear your change because they don't know how they will fit in to your new life. Will they have the same impact or hold on you? They may have to change the way they interact with you and treat you and it may also impact and re-define their role within your life. This can be scary for people who are not yet ready for their own positive change. Hopefully saboteurs will be minimal in your life, but it's best to recognize the behaviours of the saboteur and how to contend with them.

The saboteur is not necessarily someone who does not love or care about you; in fact they are quite the contrary. A saboteur can be the person who is the closest to you; a partner, spouse, child, parent, colleague, etc. When you undertake a shift in beliefs and perceptions, those close to you who may have had a hand in forming those beliefs and perceptions may feel threatened. They may take your break from their beliefs as a personal affront to them or their culture, traditions and so on. People form a way of behaving around people they know well or are close to and the behaviour may be long standing. Their roles within your life, even dysfunctional ones, have been defined with patterns of behaviour that he or she has adjusted to and feel comfortable with. For example, when you have a parent who is an addict and has had a dysfunctional way of behaving, often times the family will have to re-define their traditional roles. The parent may become more like a child in their addictive behaviour and the spouse and children will have to take over the parenting, or the partner becomes more like a parent to their spouse. The household routines change completely. This may go on for years, to the point where those people taking care of the addict have long settled into their new roles, adjusting to their new way of life. It then becomes 'normal' for the child to take on the parent role; dictating what happens in the household, being responsible for decision making, and gaining more independent and mature behaviours that are well beyond their developmental stage. The addicted parent then gets 'clean' for a period of time and begins to take back the role that the child may have taken on. There becomes conflict as the parent struggles to regain their authority, and the child rebels against having to relinquish their more independent role as they go back to having no authority and being treated as a child.

The new and improved ex-addict may see themselves as evolved and can attempt to exert their former authority maybe with a bit more enlightenment. You may then hear a partner, for example, say something like, "I liked you better when you were drinking", or "Oh why don't you go have a drink". Although this is sabotaging behaviour, it may be the significant other's natural reaction to being pushed back into their original role. This may sound completely ludicrous but it happens quite often. These perceptions can and do change over time but it is easier to change perceptions and beliefs when we have some time to prepare. It is not so easy to change if change is thrust upon us.

Anytime we undergo any major change in our lives, we go through a series of stages that are more circular than linear, which is to say that we go back and forth and spend more or less time in one or more of the stages. These are called the" Stages of Change" or the "Transtheoretical Model of Change". In order to complete a change, we go through all the stages, but it may take some time and we have to personally believe it is possible. This explains some of the reasons why changing beliefs and may be so difficult at times. We first need to be aware of the change that is happening and be able to buy into the change itself.

The Transtheoretical Model of Change can benefit from having its own chapter, so I won't get too in-depth; but I will let you know the names of the stages.

The Transtheoretical Model of Change includes five stages: Precontemplative, Contemplative, Preparation or Determination, Action and Maintenance. All of these stages are tied into our belief systems and perceptions, helping us to determine how, if and when we will make change. Since your ability to transform your individual beliefs and perceptions are tied into the stages, you should be aware of what changes you are making. In order to be present and to properly counsel our clients, it is important for us counsellors/therapists to be knowledgeable of the stages of change and what stage our clients are in at any given time. It would be ineffective to use action stage strategies with a client who is in the preparation stage of change. Knowing this information is essential to providing a client with adequate help.

Being aware of your own thoughts, beliefs and perceptions is the start to becoming more present with your spirituality, other people and life in general. Keeping your mind open to different perceptions and understanding differing beliefs will not only increase your mental and physical well being, but you will also be able to manifest the life that you want. Your mind will be open to all things that enter into your life and that will benefit you and lead you to your ideal existence. You will be able to understand that even when negative things happen, those negative circumstances may be giving you something that will ultimately benefit you. To only think of the negative as negative will cause you to discard whatever meaning it also brings with it. Look for the meaning in this type of circumstance; try to look at it as having a more positive outcome and let go of the rest.

If you learn from a negative circumstance then it is no longer negative. It has given you some insight as to what you must do in the future, thus allowing you to make change. If you keep reflecting disapprovingly about the circumstance then it becomes negative energy; energy you don't learn from and does not allow you to move forward with positive change and personal growth. This type of prolonged thought pattern can manifest in mental and physical disorders, and stop you from achieving all that you desire for your life.

It is not productive to remain completely passive either. You cannot manifest your higher spiritual self without some work and awareness. To remain in an "Oh well, whatever" state of mind without looking for some meaning can also manifest in a lack of fulfilling your life goals. When we are aware of what we do, think and believe, we achieve more, not only for ourselves, but for everyone. If each one of us was aware of the impact our littering has on our environment, we would not do it. Or at the very least, we would know that what we are doing is wrong and those feelings that go along with it could produce the change that we need to live more harmoniously with others in our world.

Hiding behind excuses as to why we exhibit negative behaviours no longer holds water. When we see someone littering and we confront their behaviour, they cannot logically defend it. To say "I didn't know that littering is wrong" would be shot down in a minute because as a whole, we know that littering is wrong and also illegal. When we have more global awareness of issues we have a collective agreement that we won't accept this behaviour any longer. So from our lack of awareness and negativity we produce globally positive mindsets. In the 70's we may have gotten away with littering but it certainly is not acceptable with the masses today.

A paradigm shift in society is one way that we can and do change our perceptions and beliefs. For example, the government may implement a new law such as no smoking inside buildings. It usually will happen over a period of time so that we, as individuals, have time to absorb the information, circulate it in our minds, compare it to our belief systems and make the transition more smoothly and positively. We have time to adjust. This is the way we typically undergo change within our minds in order to make it manifest in our lives. Even most smokers will agree that it seems so foreign now in Canada to be able to smoke inside buildings and that they would not want to see that happen again. We are all benefiting from these laws even if we have to be dragged kicking and screaming into a more positive way of being; a healthier more functional way of being, for the greater good.

Yes there are negative perceptions such as smokers having their rights taken away and that the government is playing big brother and should mind its own business, but overall, the outcome is more positive and more people are quitting smoking who may not have done it before. More of us are healthier as a result. If you can see both sides of this example you have just opened your mind to different perceptions and are able to make a more informed decision for yourself.

This is true of any belief or perception that you have. If you have the ability to see some other insight or understand another principle system, you are better able to make more informed decisions based on different factors rather than on your own perspective. You will expand your mind, open yourself to more positive energy and be able to manifest what you need in your life. Through this expanded awareness and openness to change, you can discard the negative beliefs, perceptions and thoughts and become more attuned with your spiritual self. Everything that impacts you and your life will begin to change and you will become more joyous and peaceful, and feel more interconnected with the universe and all that it has to offer. When you exert positive energy, you attract positive manifestations. Your mental and physical health will start to improve, you will be able to handle conflict and stressful situations better, your living and working environments will be more inviting and your overall outlook on life will be more optimistic.

Take your ego out of your active, day to day thinking as much as possible and you will begin to realize that you are a much more powerful human being than you think. Many of the most powerful people in history were not ego driven in the least; Mother Teresa, The Dhali Lama, Ghandi. Think of the people in your life, or who you have met in your life, that has had the most positive impact on you simply with their presence. Were these egotistical people? Probably not, but they were no doubt powerful. They draw you in and you want to be close to them physically because they give off such an optimistic and powerful energy; a sense of peacefulness that does not seem to exist in the masses as yet. I am hopeful that this too will change. We are starting to see that paradigm shift in society where people are beginning to recognize that we are all capable of manifesting positive change and becoming closer to living in our spiritual essence.

Aligning your spiritual self with your human existence is not so hard to do if you are willing to put forth the effort. It is mainly fear that stops us from moving forward. Fear that if we change our belief systems and perceptions, we will not know how to function and we will be seen differently by those who are in our lives. Any change can be scary if that is how you view it. I would ask you to change your perception to one of excitement; the same excitement that a child has when they are embarking on a new adventure. When you change the way you think and view things, you change the emotions that are attached to the thought or circumstance. We become fearful due in part to our belief systems, such as "I am too old to change my career", or "I have never been able to do that, therefore I will fail if I try". Remember that some of your belief systems have been with you since childhood and no longer relate to who you are now, or what you are capable of. Those beliefs may be untrue but yet you hang onto them as if they are. When you were five you may not have been able to ride a bike, but you can certainly learn to do it now if you put your positive mind to it. Certainly rock climbing was not a part of our regular society thirty years ago, but now many people are doing it, even in urban settings.

Our world has changed, and we have changed, but we manage to hang onto negative mindset regardless of how different we are now. Go through your storage area of beliefs and perceptions and de-clutter. You can then shape your life according to the new knowledge that you bring in. You will have the room to expand your mind and your life and you will have more room for your spiritual being. You will start to see life differently and many opportunities may be presented to you, if you have the awareness to see them.

Like I mentioned previously, fear is the basis of our unwillingness to change. Fear that people will not accept the new you, or like the new you, or that somehow you will lose all that you have gained so far. Creating room for positive growth and change will only enhance your life. You will be able to manifest the life that you could only have previously imagined. Sure there may be people in your life that feel fearful or threatened by your new positive and spiritual self, but you must remember those people who would bring negativity to something that is positive are themselves stuck in negative energy and ego based thinking ; they are not truly there to enhance your life. You may end up discarding people in your life that are unwilling to support you, or are only concerned about you staying with their negativity so that they have someone to shovel the garbage with.

Outgrowing people that have been part of your life is something that happens all the time. Rarely do we have all the same friends in our life that we had in kindergarten. Most of us meet new people and lose track of others through our journey. But as one door closes, another one opens. If someone is not supportive of you, perhaps out of their own fear, and want to keep you at their level of negativity, it is important for you to look at the relationship you have with that person and understand how they have fit into your life in the past and what purpose they will have in the future.

It can be scary to end a relationship because you are uncertain of their reaction or are scared you won't meet new people. Most of us do not want to be alone for the rest of our lives and some people say "better the devil you know". This is such a false belief because when you align your spiritual self with positive energy and are willing to change negative beliefs and perceptions, you open doors allowing positive people, opportunities and relationships to come into your life. View these as new and exciting adventures. Fear of the unknown will be replaced with renewed vigour, increased energy and life changing experiences. Just like the first time you did something new; a new sport or game, job or learning to drive, you didn't know what to expect but you did it anyway. Now you know what to expect and it's not so scary anymore.

The negative people in your life will learn quickly that they should change their ways or not have you in their lives. Once the initial cynicism is over, most people will begin to ask questions about your new way of being and perhaps start to change themselves. It is normal to expect some resistance from others because they will be contemplating if change is good for them too. Some people in your life may feel they don't have a place in your "new" life. Give them the knowledge you have, pass on the book you've read or the phone number of the counsellor you have seen, or name of the place where you received help, and then just wait and see what happens. If they are not yet ready for change proceed without them down your path. It is your path alone to walk so enjoy the journey; there will be many wonders to experience along the way.

In this chapter we have looked at the ways in which you can change your perceptions, beliefs and thoughts so that you can expand your mind to accepting more positive change. I hope I have provided you with a clearer understanding of how beliefs and perceptions mould us and our behaviours.

We have also taken a look at some of the pitfalls that your positive change may evoke as you proceed down your path to positive change. We looked at the saboteurs specifically and the characteristics that they display. We have also linked some spiritual aspects of the positive change and the outcomes that follow, including: increased peace, joy, connection to our spiritual selves, and the positive impact on mental and physical health.

Remember that as with any new behaviour and change, you may stumble a few times, but the key is to go easy on yourself (don't kick yourself for not being able to change immediately). Change is a process so stick to it. Fear impacts our beliefs and perceptions and this chapter will help you choose to distinguish change as a positive, new and exciting adventure in your life!

This is only the beginning and positive change should be a lifelong journey. Ask questions and gain information in any way that appeals to you (workshops, seminars, read books, seek the help of a counsellor or other professionals, watch programs that are in line with the new behaviours that you want to achieve, etc) because personal and spiritual growth is ongoing and comes in many different forms. Choose the path to improvement that is right for you.

CHAPTER 3

COMMUNICATION

We all have the ability to communicate. Even those who are considered deaf, mute and have no ability to move, have the ability to communicate. I have worked with people who could only move their eyebrows or eyes and make sounds, and I was not only able to communicate with them but understand their personalities, likes, dislikes, what their needs were and even their sense of humour. It was a matter of closing my internal chatter, observing their behaviours and non-verbal responses and being completely present for them.

Most of our communication is non-verbal (body language and facial expressions). I have been fortunate enough to be educated in augmentative communication and neurolinguistic programming, which is the technical jargon for all non-verbal types of communication. I am fascinated by the ability we have as humans to have our needs met via the ways in which we communicate. How we communicate really does speak volumes about the type of people we are, whether it is verbal or non-verbal.

Our listening skills are a huge part of our communication as well. I find that many people do not engage in active listening. Active listening is a skill that is really not taught in schools and yet has a great impact in how we interact with others. Many clients that I have worked with stated that their biggest issues involved not feeling heard, or feeling like they have no voice. The issue of poor communication is prevalent throughout society. It affects our self esteem and emotional health. It can be the difference between a good relationship and a bad one, and may be responsible for many separations and divorces.

In this chapter I will outline how to engage in active listening skills and ways in which we don't listen but think we are. I will also help you to identify ways in which your communication style may be doing you damage and how to repair it. You can become more effective in your work and personal life by changing the way in which you communicate. The way you communicate speaks volumes about who you are. I'm not talking about your vocabulary or how many words you know, but about how to effectively let others know what you would like to convey. Whether it is to get your needs met, or teaching colleagues about the latest advances in your business, you need to communicate in a way that allows another person to fully understand the message you are trying to put forth.

Quite often we say one thing but our body language says another. Most of us can pick up on stronger variances between spoken language and body language. Your brain has difficulty betraying what you are thinking or feeling and usually will give your inner intentions away in spite of the words that come out of your mouth. Your gut will attempt to tell you that something does not match even before your conscious thought has a chance to pick up on it.

For example, you may get a feeling that the person speaking to you is not being truthful, or is hiding something but you just can't put your finger on it. Your gut has already determined that something is incongruent between what the person is saying and how they are acting (their body language or non-verbal communication). Their tone of voice may say that they are angry, hurt, excited, etc. but their words are portraying another message entirely. We will be looking at some, but not all, of the elements of communication that can get us into difficulties as well as how to engage in healthy communication styles.

From the time we are born we start communicating. Yes, we actually start communicating while in the womb, but for our purposes we will look at post birth communication. Upon taking our first breath we cry out and let everyone within earshot know that you have arrived and are alive. I should acknowledge that there are newborns who do not cry out when they take their first breath, but the majority do. Newborns and infants are among the best communicators, are they not? We as parents are highly in tune with the cry of our newborn. Without speaking a word they get all of their needs met. They get nourishment, warmth, comfort and have their human waste disposed of. They let us know when they are awake, tired, hungry, dirty, uncomfortable or unhealthy, agitated, angry, happy, etc. and we respond accordingly. What little masterminds they are. And then they learn words.

But before we even learn words, we learn to communicate by observing the behaviours of others and mimicking it. A child may not understand how to interpret the behaviour but he or she can certainly copy it. Children then attempt to interpret the behaviour, but only according to his or her developmental stage and brain maturity at the time. It would be wonderful if every behaviour we observed was healthy and positive but, as human beings, this is not always the way. For example, if you drink alcohol to excess, it can certainly be an eye opener when your four year old comes over to you with a drink in his or her hand, says that they are imitating you, and then starts acting outrageously.

In our attempt to educate them, we say that it is alcohol and that it's okay for adults to drink it but that it is harmful to children. The immature mind may interpret this to mean that you are hurting yourself, or that if you are okay when you drink alcohol, then they will be okay if they drink it, regardless of what words you are saying. This can create a host of emotions for the child, including fear, shame, indifference, or the thought that they have done something wrong depending on how the adult deals with the situation. The adult could go even further to engage the child in other unhealthy behaviour such as covering up the incident or having the child 'keep secrets' from the other parent which then teaches the child that these unhealthy behaviours are acceptable and sometimes even encouraged. Our children are little vacuums and take in all kinds of information from their environment, even if they can't speak. In turn, the child learns to incorporate this behaviour into his or her communication style.

It is imperative that we stop and think about the messages, verbal and non-verbal, that we are sending. We think about our outside appearance by making sure our personal style, fashion, hair and make-up are sending a clear message about who we are but often times we don't take the same care and diligence to ensure that our verbal and non-verbal communication are presented to give the same message. We may even work on one facet of our oral communication by making sure we speak in an even tone or with enough vocal intensity so that everyone in the room can hear us, but then we use language that gives off subtle (or not so subtle) messages of negativity or aggressiveness or even a sense of insecurity. By being mindful of our positive energy and honour, we can tailor our communication so we send out only messages that will bring back positive energy and thus be able to manifest what we want into our lives.

The use of negative statements is one of the ways we subconsciously send out negative energy when in fact we want to portray a positive message. We then wonder why we are receiving negative responses. The example that I will use here is the use of the word 'fight'. We say that we are committed to the fight for the rights of one group or another. The cause may be worth going to bat for but the message is sending out negative energy. More positive and peace filled messages will go farther to help a cause than the aggressive evoking negative statements. Instead use positive statements such as 'our commitment to helping raise awareness for this noble cause will help us to find a cure', rather than 'we are fighting against this disease and will stop at nothing to find a cure'. A subtle change of frequency will be sent out to whomever you are speaking to, and will be embedded in each message. Each message has a high degree of passion for the speaker but will impact the outcomes.

Positive statements and positive energy bring about positive results.

Change the way in which you speak by being aware of the words that you use. One of the more popular statements that we hear on a daily basis is 'I can't...' We must take ownership over what we say; the proper choice of statements should be 'I choose not to...', or 'I choose to do this instead'. When you say that you 'cannot' do something what that really means is that you are physically unable to do it. Most of the time, this statement is false. Be clear about what you are choosing to do and not do and this in turn will bring your personal power back to you. This also gives the person you are speaking with a clear message of your intent. You can then give a positive statement as to what you are prepared to do, if anything.

Rather than giving a negative self statement, such as "I look too fat in this..." change it to a positive statement, such as "I am a beautiful person, inside and out". Positive self talk may seem silly to some of you at first but you will learn over time to view things more positively and refer to the positive when speaking in general. Positive self talk will also improve your self-esteem!

It is stated that, on average, we make 20,000 choices during the course of our day. Most of those choices are made subconsciously. Could you imaging if we had to think about each choice we made? We would probably accomplish very little. Most of our choices have been programmed into our brain through repetition. I am asking you to be more mindful of the choices that you make, especially the ones that make you feel negative inside.

Most of us have had to do things that make us feel negative inside, such as completing a task for your employer that you may not agree with, or completing chores at home that you may not find fulfilling, but none the less must be done. It is okay to do something that you don't agree with as long as it still goes along with your core values. You may be asked to stay late at work to finish a major project. While this may be inconvenient, it does not impact your core values, such as integrity, honesty, trust, respect, honour, etc. Indeed while it may be inconvenient, it may also bolster your core values. If you finish the project on deadline, you will have a greater sense of pride, integrity, self respect, dignity, etc.

If you are asking someone to stay late at work, you may want to ask a more positive question rather than say a negative statement. One example of this is, "Can you stay late tonight to help us finish this project?" Rather than, "You'll need to stay late tonight to finish this project." This positive statement will give the power back to the person who is being asked and in turn provide more of an onus on the person to take personal responsibility for their work. The latter statement tends to evoke more negative feelings and often the person being told what to do will take less personal responsibility for the work and feel more negative towards the situation. The former statement, while evoking more ownership, will also create more of a sense of increased core values such as the ones mentioned previously.

When we are more aware of the choices that we make, we can change the negative communication to positive and gain better results, while keeping our core values intact. An employer who bullies workers into doing their jobs will find that he has workers who are less productive and take more sick time or time off. Quite often, there tends to be more theft of company property as well as high staff turnover. The boss in turn gains a negative reputation, not only as a bad employer, but also as a bad person. He may eventually only be able to attract the less skilled people who plan on using his business as a transitional job only. Everyone suffers. He most likely will also lose customers and his business is more likely to fail.

Try to speak in positives. When you are aware of what you are saying you will be able to identify the negative wording and change them in to positive statements. By looking at the opposite wording of a negative statement you can usually come up with the positive statement. For example, "I hate when it rains" can be stated as "I prefer sunshine to rain", or "We really need this rain to help the plants grow". By stating a negative you are putting out negative thoughts and energy. You will only bring back into your life the negative energy you put out. Negative thought patterns do lead to a negative mindset and cause negative actions. Subconsciously we make choices based on our energy and mindset. Like I mentioned previously in the perception and belief chapter, our mindsets are borne from our beliefs and perceptions. We need to be cognizant of what drives our choices, including our thoughts and emotions. How many times have we given in to our children's demands because we're exhausted? Most parents will be able to relate to that.

Since our communication abilities extend beyond verbal communication, we must think about what we are saying to others with our minds and body language. What does your body language and non-verbal communication say about you? Do you hang your head and look at the ground more often than not, or do you hold your head up and make eye contact with others? It might not seem like a big deal but these simple behaviours speak volumes about you. Holding your head up and making eye contact with others is a positive behaviour as opposed to hanging your head and avoiding eye contact which sends a negative message to others that you lack self esteem and are somehow "not worthy". It can also speak to depression, anxiety and stress. It can be very difficult to change a negative behaviour when it is tied into core beliefs and perceptions that are ingrained and long standing, but as you learn to unravel the stream of negative behaviours, beliefs and perceptions, you can change negative communication into positive communication, even if you're still in the process of changing long standing ingrained behaviours.

It is not essential for you to change your negative beliefs and perceptions entirely in order to start changing negative communication patterns. It comes down to awareness of what you are communicating to others. Over 80% of what you say to others is said through facial expressions alone. The tone of your voice and the energy you put into your statements can also be changed to reflect more positive energy. Sincerity and empathy also play into your communication patterns. We can say that we are sorry that something has happened, but if we don't communicate that in the tone of our voice or the sincerity with which we say it, others will detect that you are not heartfelt in your statement.

All too often I hear people apologizing either for things they should not be apologizing for, or as a way of being able to engage in negative behaviour over and over again. I'm sure most of us have at some point heard someone say they are sorry with an almost sing-song aspect to it. They are upbeat in their tone and their facial expressions often denote happiness as they are often smiling while singing sor-ry. It's as if they use the word sorry as a way of distracting people from their behaviour or statements. If you're not sincere with what you say to others you might as well save your breath and not say anything. When you fake an apology, you just might be creating more bad feelings by being insincere and unaccountable for your behaviours.

When people apologize for no reason, I will ask them why they are apologizing. Once the question is asked, that person will usually give it some thought and then realize that they did not need to apologize. It is also difficult to receive an apology as sincere when you know that the person will apologize for just about anything, including the weather or other things that they have no control over. We need to really think about what we are going to say and say what we mean before we say it.

The way you relay negative information doesn't have to be negative and nasty. You can be much more effective about relaying any information if you come from a positive perspective. Let's face it, we are going to have negative information and situations in our lives, but we can manage the way in which we communicate that information or situation. Remember that we must always honour our spiritual selves as well as others. We do not want to choose to create a situation for ourselves that will take our positive power away from us. So when you say you're sorry, be sure you mean it; express it, both facially and in your tone. Take responsibility and be accountable for your actions and behaviours. It won't serve you well to be laughing and smiling as you attempt to apologize for hurting another human being. Apologize when it is necessary and others will take your apology as meaningful and sincere, rather than another word in your vocabulary.

When communicating, many people tend to be reactionary, that is to say we match the tone, pitch and speed of the person who we are reacting to. This type of communication can easily spiral out of control in negative situations. It can work well in positive situations, such as a friend announcing their engagement, but it can also work well in negative situations, such as arguments. We hear in the news quite often that someone has been injured or killed because of an argument, fight, or some perceived disrespect. "He looked at me wrong and I beat him up for it". Often times, we may not even be aware of what we are communicating to others just by looking at someone or something.

When we react to someone in a negative situation, the process generally starts from a feeling in our gut and that will signal the fight or flight system in our brains to prepare us for what is to come next. Our breathing becomes more rapid, our pupils dilate, our veins dilate to allow more blood flow and our adrenaline kicks in to high gear. At the same time our brains are preparing our bodies for fight or flight, we tend to lack in other areas, such as listening, and will only assess visually what is going on, reading body language and non-verbal language without actively listen to what the person is trying to tell us. This is why it is almost futile to try to have a conversation with someone when they are angry. They are focused on their anger and the situation which caused them to choose to react in an angry manner, not with what you are saying. If we engage in behaviours that match those of the other person, this will serve to escalate the already negative behaviour; neither person gets heard and we pull negative energy to us at an alarming speed.

Like any other emotion, anger is valuable to us. It acts as a barometer when situations challenge our morals, principles, beliefs, security and mores. We could not know what joy or happiness feels like if we did not have anger to compare it to. Just like any other emotion, anger has its place. It just happens to be one of those emotions that can have devastating and deadly effects if not harnessed properly. Anger has a lot of power and energy that comes with it. Anger can also be used in a way that communicates strength and action. If we channel our anger to elicit change then anger is used in a positive way that brings with it positive energy. The way in which we communicate anger will greatly affect the outcome of the situation.

When we scream and yell, pound our fists or stomp our feet we are unleashing a wave of negative energy to the universe that undoubtedly will come back to us in much the same way as it went out. We also let others know that we have closed our minds to differing views or perceptions. We send out a loud message that we are not concerned with creating a win-win situation but instead must be found to be right. We can definitely get our needs met temporarily but will not gain in the long run. Relationships suffer, work and social performance deteriorate as negative energy will abound and affect every aspect of life, including mental and physical health.

If we are able to be aware of what is making us angry, as well as our own beliefs around the particular situation that makes us angry, we can then choose to see a different perspective so that the anger can be directed in a more positive way. Every day it seems, we hear that another child has been senselessly and needlessly murdered. I think that most of us would agree that the parents of those murdered children have every right to be angry. There are those who will be consumed by the anger and grief and lash out at the murderers, while others will be consumed in anger but will turn their anger and grief inward and become depressed. Still we see others who are able to forgive the murderers and champion legal change or worthy causes as a way of harnessing their anger. The latter will produce more positive energy and become a productive way for those to manage their anger and be able to move forward with their lives.

When we understand how and why a negative situation comes about, we are better able to assess what needs to be done to rectify the situation and develop more options for ourselves. Even if we might not ever know how or why a situation developed, we can still choose to accept and create positive change. It will only help us to exert positive energy as the alternative can be devastating. We don't fault those who cannot move past their anger in this situation, we instead send out loving, positive energy to them in whatever way that suits; prayer, donations, support, blessings, etc.

Communicating is much more than what we say. It is how we act, react, make decisions, dress, eat, carry ourselves and judge situations. I can go on and on because everything we say, think and do communicates much about ourselves to the rest of the world. We have even been told that through scientific studies there is evidence that our cells and organs communicate with those who are particularly connected to us. We need to pay attention to our communication patterns.

ACTIVE LISTENING

A great deal of our interactive communication with others depends on our active listening skills. We can make or break relationships according to how well we listen, or don't listen to others. One of the biggest issues that many of my clients face is they don't feel listened to, heard, or that they feel that they have no voice in their relationships with others. We all fall into the pit of faulty listening skills at times. For example, when you're tired or in a negative mood, busy, stressed or have other things on your mind your listening skills may not be 'up to par'. But if you stay connected with the present moment you can significantly increase you ability to actively listen to another person and thus change the nature of the relationship itself, from one of lack, to one of presence.

When the person that you are in a conversation with recognizes that you are present for them when they are speaking with you, they respond more positively to you, and your conversations become more meaningful, as does the relationship itself.

Not only will your conversations become more meaningful, but your relationships become more enhanced, there is less resentment (because those who feel unheard do become resentful of those who are not listening to them). Others will feel more respected by you if you truly and actively listen to what they are saying, not to mention that when you are truly present for someone else in a conversation, you come across as being interested in that person and this will elevate their esteem as well.

It sounds simple to say 'stay present' for your conversations with others, but it can become easier said than done at times, especially given the mental states we can find ourselves in that were mentioned earlier. Throughout this book I have stated that cultivating a mindset of living in the present as much as possible is one of the most authentic ways of being. Again, you must move to action to attain goals but once you have set that agenda, you should stay present for every step of your way.

I am going to outline some of the ways in which we do not listen actively and you may recognize some of the pitfalls. As you begin to recognize the pitfalls that trip you up, you will begin to understand and implement active listening skills.

One of the pitfalls of our listening skills is **inadequate or distracted listening.** This type of listening skill involves being easily distracted from what others are saying to you. One of the most common examples of inadequate listening is thinking about other things that are not related to the conversation, "what do I need to do later", |did I forget something", becoming preoccupied with what is going on in our own heads. By becoming aware of our own internal dialogue, we can then turn it off and shift back to the other person and what they are saying.

Sometimes we become too eager to respond that we miss some of the conversation and end up minimizing what the other person has to say. When you become too eager you can tend to get caught up in your own experiences that are similar to what is being said by the other person, and turn the conversation around to become about you. Pay attention to what others are saying and make a quick mental note of what you wanted to interject. You can then come back to it when the other person has finished what they are saying. If you are present for the conversation you don't have to worry about forgetting what it is you wanted to say.

Another pitfall to active listening is **evaluative listening**. When you engage in evaluative listening, you tend to judge what the other person is saying in terms of whether the information is right or wrong, good or bad, relevant or irrelevant to you, acceptable or unacceptable, and so on. You must remember that you are evaluating the conversation based on your individual belief systems, so try to remember this and keep an open mind.

This does not mean that you cannot interject your own belief systems to the conversation but if you listen to fully understand the conversation, then and only then do you gain awareness and insight. This can help you understand a differing point of view, which in turn can expand your mind and your life, as well as shatter some unhealthy belief systems of your own.

This brings us to one of the pitfalls that most of us engage in, which is **filtered listening**. Filtered listening is more about our personal belief systems and perceptions which can create bias to listening. These biases come from our own personal, familial, sociological, economical, religious and cultural beliefs that form filters to actively and openly listening to other conversations.

Most of us can relate to the feelings that we just don't identify with the person who may be speaking to us. It may be difficult at times to actively listen to someone who you know may have prejudices or someone who lives in a completely different world than you do. Although it may seem painful at times to listen to someone who is boring to us, try to expand your mind and relate. Remember, we are interconnected and we all have much to contribute to the world. You may even find yourself being able to identify with that person on a much more human or even spiritual level. New and exciting things may come as a result of taking the time to actively listen.

Cheryl Hitchcock

One other pitfall that needs to be noted stems from filtered listening; labels as **filters.** We can distort our listening by putting labels on people and conversations. Take a minute to think of how you would listen to someone if you knew that they had a mental illness such as schizophrenia, or someone who is a famous athlete or movie star. It is easy to pigeonhole people when we know about their labels. We tend to assign plusses or minuses to the worth of their conversations as well as them, because of their labels. Whether you tend to value someone more or less still creates a filter on the conversation and prevents us from actively listening. Think about this the next time you meet someone new and start a conversation. Don't ask what they do for a living, where they are from, what kind of car they drive, or their educational background. This may sound tough because most of us tend to gravitate towards these types of questions when we first meet someone. Try instead to engage them in a conversation about a mutual seminar you are both taking, or complementing them on an aspect of their clothing. Or stick to a neutral topic such as the weather. This may take away a filter that has been with you for some time. Then when you do gain information about the previous topics, gauge if you've changed how you feel about that person.

Take away the labels and engage with others for the simple sake of engaging with another human being. The art of conversation can be quite exhilarating if we move to a place where we are present and engaged with each other. We're all having this human experience together and you can learn so much from removing the barriers by simply listening.

We also tend to think about what our own response to the conversation will be. We tend to **rehearse** our responses in our head while the other person is still talking. When you rehearse the next thing you are going to say, you can't possibly be listening to the conversation actively. If you are actively listening to a person, a natural flow of conversation tends to occur. This rehearsing prevents us from hearing the true meaning of a conversation. A husband might start to determine that he will be in trouble when he returns home late or has missed an important function. He may begin to rehearse his reasons before the conversation starts. As the rehearsal continues throughout his conversation with his wife, she begins to escalate in her frustration at not being listened to. You may well prevent some embarrassing statements if you listen actively to what is being said.

This type of scenario can also be true for **fact based** listening. When we only listen to facts, and not to the person who is speaking, we tend to miss a lot of the conversation. It is important to listen to the person contextually. It is great to get all the facts but then you can miss the person's point entirely. This can also lead to labels and filtering of conversation.

The last pitfall to actively listening is **interrupting.** As soon as you interrupt another person you are not listening anymore. Certainly there are times when you need to interrupt a person, say for example, when you cannot hear what they are saying, or you missed a portion of the conversation, or if you are giving minimal responses such as 'I agree' or 'okay' or 'uh-huh', but these responses are ones that allow the other person to recognize that you are listening to the conversation.

The kind of interruption that I am speaking about is the kind that derails the other person from what they were saying, as well as minimizing what the other person had to say. Since interrupting can be construed as being rude and disrespectful, we should not do it. This is the one pitfall of active listening that we can recognize and be aware of more easily since it stops the other person from speaking. If we need to interrupt for something important or to add to a monologue of sorts, it's quite acceptable to just say, "Excuse me for the interruption but..." or "can I interrupt for just a moment, I wanted to add something to what you just said before the conversation moves too far along". These examples are conscientious interruptions that are more benign. Interruptions that are done for no considerate reason, such as when someone comes into a conversation that has already started and starts speaking about another subject entirely, or if someone changes the subject in the middle of what someone else is saying are unacceptable.

You need to allow a person to say what they are going to say in its entirety so that you can fully understand what is being said. I have seen this time and again from professionals sitting in clinical meetings. One person is attempting to fill in the team about a subject and others just start interrupting to give advice as to what you should do before you have a chance to tell them what you have already done. I know this happens in everyday conversations as well.

Now that you can recognize the pitfalls of actively listening, you can begin the process to being a wonderful listener instead of hearing "you never listen to me".

There are ways in which you can improve your listening skills and genuinely engage with others through your verbal and non-verbal communication.

You can **maintain eye contact** with the person who is speaking to you so that they know you are present. You can also **reflect back** on what they've said so that the person knows that you are not only listening but able to understand his or her perspective. For example, you could say, "So, what you're saying is..." Summarize what you've heard in case of any misinterpretations or when listing things. This may sound like a lot to do when having a conversation but it isn't. You don't necessarily need to reflect or summarize a conversation to a stranger or during a casual conversation about the weather; however, when speaking with someone whom you have a relationship with and have had negative feedback about your ability to listen well, you may want to try these easy strategies. You will see the benefits instantly...

If we look at the spirituality aspect of our communication with others, we understand that much of our conversations take place without the use of words but with a sense of inter-connectedness with our fellow human beings. You have the ability to transfer your energy to another person and direct the path of their energy. We've all had incidences where we come into contact with another person and feel and see their misery before they have a chance to utter a word. This often has an immediate effect on us and our decision to approach or even speak with that person.

Be aware of this energy transfer during your meetings with others so that if negative energy comes your way, you can divert to positive, kind and loving thoughts for that person. You can change the course of their energy, before their misery sucks you in and leaves you feeling negative or drained.

Of course, energy transfer works both ways; negative or positive. You may find yourself drawn to people who exhibit positive energy. Their work, home and social lives thrive and they are genuinely supportive and trustworthy people. They can communicate more effectively and they truly are present in their conversations with others. You might say that this type of person shows a genuine interest in the people with whom they are communicating.

Understanding and recognizing that we are all interconnected and divine human beings can go a long way in understanding healthy communication, and the type of energy we put out to others. The average person can affect approximately 300 people in a day. That's not to say that you necessarily speak with 300 people per day, but you come into energy contact with that many. If you can spread positive energy throughout your day, you can positively affect many others. These people that you have affected with your positive energy and positive, non verbal communication (a smile or nod) will then come into contact with, on average, 300 more people, and so on and so on. So you see, the more positive thoughts, deeds and energy you spread, the more positive all of us become. You truly have the ability to affect others, so my advice is to use it for positive outcomes. It will help you to live a better life and help those around you, who may be having a less than wonderful day, to feel a little more cheer.

CHAPTER 4

SELF-ESTEEM

Who among us has never suffered from low self esteem at some point in life? I see people daily who are adamant that they have a good healthy sense of self esteem. They then set out to prove it in unhealthy, dysfunctional ways. Make no mistake; there is a difference between being arrogant or conceited and having a good healthy sense of worth.

Self-esteem is defined as the way in which you think of yourself; your own value and abilities. It is quite often tied into our sense of self worth and self consciousness. It is the way in which we identify ourselves and the impact these thoughts have on our lives and the decisions we make.

Our positive and negative thoughts and views are quite often developed in early childhood and at first come from outside sources. As we develop, we keep and discard certain beliefs and statements that are made (i.e. "You're a pretty girl if only you could lose/gain some weight. " "Why can't you figure this out, are you stupid?" or "You have an awful attitude!" etc.). Over time these comments affect the way we see and define ourselves and our worth in the world. These comments become ingrained in us and affect every aspect of our lives. We can learn to manage some of these issues and overcome others (with work).

There is work involved in identifying self-esteem and self worth issues. Self-esteem issues are deep-rooted and become part of our psyche and personality. We integrate these issues to a point of being comfortable with them, thus allowing achievement and success, but only to a certain point. We need to bring these issues to the surface, identify how they affect us and our decisions, as well as the impact they have on us and our lives. Seeking the help of a professional can be beneficial for this part of the work.

Fear is usually at the basis of any significant change and prevents us from moving on in a more positive and dynamic way. We minimize, deny and repress our fears but they surface in our behaviours and decisions. To deny the issues that keep you from achieving is to deny success. We "make due with" or "settle for" mediocrity. Remember that profound change and vast success means stepping outside your comfort zone.

Your self-esteem may be negative or low but it is what you know and feel comfortable with. People in general are reluctant to work and live outside their comfort zones, even if the behaviours are destructive to them and their self esteem. When fear is at the basis of this, your self esteem issues are what holds you back from change and achieving your ultimate success.

Identify the fear! This is the basis of your barriers. When you identify your fears, you are better able to identify what you need to do to overcome them. If the fear of rejection is part of your reluctance to change, remember that rejection is a normal part of moving forward in life. Thomas Edison was rejected over 2000 times before he was able to go ahead with his invention of the electric light bulb. The key is persistence and an unwavering belief in yourself and your success.

One of the most difficult fears for us to understand is the fear of success! Now you may be thinking that success is what you are striving for so it's silly to think that your desired goal is what you fear the most. Well this fear is real and it is prevalent in our society. Have you ever heard anyone say they don't want success in some area of their life? Most likely not. Most of us say that we want success in some, if not all, areas of our life. But when it comes down to making it a goal and working towards it, we do some of the nuttiest things to sabotage our own success. Why? Because we are then forced to look at our own self esteem issues that have been bogging us down. We may not even be able to identify how we are self sabotaging, but we easily come up with reasons why we are not achieving the success we are seeking. We put up barriers and then say that if only that barrier was not there, we could be successful.

We are the masters of our own destiny and therefore the masters of our own healing. It is up to you to gain awareness of the personal self esteem and self worth issues that are preventing you from achieving the success you envision for yourself. Awareness, as always, is the first step in changing any behaviour. Others may be able to identify your self esteem issues, but unless you become aware of and actively seek information to understand these issues, you may never be able to identify them. It takes trust to ask a close friend to assess your self esteem challenges so I urge you to seek the help of a professional to uncover your particular issues. But remember; don't assume that your most trusted friend does not want to support you as you seek help. You may wish to still include a friend or close family member in your self-learning process

Identifying your unique issues that directly affect your self esteem will take work. Following strategies can make it easier for you. Since this can be an emotionally painful process, I suggest you solicit the help of a professional in this field. You may not yet be able to recognize your self esteem challenges at this point in your life. These issues may have cropped up long ago and are buried so deep you have no way of recognizing them yet.

Seeking the help of a professional counsellor or therapist is integral to identifying your issues, so let go of the stigma of seeking assistance. You wouldn't think twice about seeking professional help for any number of other issues such as physical health, financial investments, educational pursuits, resume writing and job skills, etc. Seeking the help and guidance of a professional who will be objective, insightful and give you the direction you need to put your life on a positive, healthy track and solve negative life issues is just as valuable as having a good family doctor. We need to get over the fact that if a person seeks help for issues pertaining to the mind or psyche, they are mentally ill. This would make the majority of us on earth mentally ill, and we are not. These are mental (meaning mind) health issues but in no way are they linked to being mentally ill or having a psychiatric diagnosis. People who are aware of this factor are better able to keep the mind and body in pique condition and are proven to lead more peaceful, happier lives. Who wouldn't want that?

Here are some strategies you can use to identify your self esteem issues, in order to help you get on the path to a positive sense of self:

- Try to identify the areas that are affecting your self-esteem and sense of self-worth. (What are your internal voices saying to you?)

- Take inventory of your internal messages that tie into your self-esteem and self-worth (Are they true?) Some of them have been there for life and put there by someone else.

- Identify the fears and barriers to your success (one of the more popular fears is the fear of success!)

- Write a list of your positive attributes in all aspects of your life.

- Write a list of goals that you have envisioned but did not think were achievable based on your old patterns of self esteem.

- Write out a timeline and specific steps to take to achieve those goals now.

- Share your goals with someone you trust and who will check in with you to help motivate and keep you on track.

Take ownership, responsibility and accountability for your goals and success. When you do this, you will have yourself to thank and give a big pat on the back to. The sense of self pride is enormous.

Remember – you need to invest in yourself, not only on the outside through physical fitness, but also in your mind. Your mind drives everything that you do, and it needs to be given priority.

One thing that you may need to tackle on the way to achieving increased self esteem is the common belief that we all must be modest and humble. I'm not saying you should turn into an arrogant, conceited person, but you can confidently blow your own horn in a kind and loving way. When we speak from a place of loving kindness about ourselves, it comes through to others differently than if we speak from a place of arrogance or low self esteem. Our voices sound different, in addition to our facial expressions, body language and energy.

Take time out from your busy life to improve yourself and yourself esteem. You really do deserve to believe in yourself and achieve success!

CHAPTER 5

STRESS & ANXIETY

In this chapter, we will be looking at stress and anxiety as these two often go hand in hand in today's society. You will find that I use the words stress and stressor in this chapter. 'Stress' is the condition on the human body both mentally and physiologically, and 'stressor' is the event or organism that is perceived to create the stress. The way we deal with the stress is called a 'coping strategy'. Stress can and often does lead to anxiety and, if left unchecked, can create disorders such as anxiety or panic attacks.

Stress and anxiety are a part of our everyday, human experience. Who among us has not experienced some stress, or anxiety, whether it's good or bad? Yes, believe it or not, there is good stress, but it affects our body the same as bad stress does. It increases heart rate and respiration, can make us anxious, nervous or fearful and can create conditions that can be detrimental to our mental and physical health. Good stress is called 'eustress' and bad stress is called 'distress'.

Take for example, a wedding. A wedding is generally considered to be a happy occasion, but the involvement in planning and preparing for the celebration can create considerable stress and anxiety. The birth of a child, even though it is an extremely exciting time, can create the most profound fear and worry, causing stress and anxiety.

When we understand stress and anxiety, we can better manage it so that it does not affect our mental or physical health in devastating ways. It can ultimately lead to death if left to fester out of control. Our society today exposes us to a number of stressful events in any given day. If we don't find a healthy way to cope then the stress and anxiety can accumulate until our body will finally say 'that's enough' and will begin a process of breaking down or shutting down. Our stress hormones will be released and will remain even after the stressor is gone. We may start to feel uneasy but not be sure why. We may start to lose or gain an appetite, lose sleep, and become irritable, depressed, short tempered or even hostile, among other things. None of which will help ease the nervous tension but in fact do the opposite, adding even more stress. Even perceived stress of a non-threatening stressor has the same effect on our brains and bodies.

In order to temporarily fix the situation, some of us may resort to a myriad of unhealthy behaviours to cope with our stress or anxiety. For example, if you are a social drinker and like the feeling you get from alcohol, you may decide to drink more when feeling nervous and anxious; enjoying the numbing effects that accompany alcohol use. While this may be effective in forgetting about the situation, or repressing your feelings, this is only temporary. The situation that first caused the maladaptive coping strategy is still there and continues to gain in strength. The only thing that happens as a result of the negative coping strategy of drinking, for example, is that you now have to deal with another potential stressor and that is the alcohol issue and its cumulative effects, in addition to the original source of stress or anxiety.

There are some people who are more predisposed to stress and anxiety than others. We gauge the severity of stress in one's life based on what degree it disrupts their everyday functioning. For example, if someone is stressed to the point of not being able to concentrate or focus on a task, and work is disrupted because of this, then the stress is significant. Especially if one is fired from work due to poor job performance.

The nature of the stressor is also important; how long you are exposed to the stressor, what cumulative effects prolonged stress has on you, how many stressors an individual faces at one time, or when a known stressor (such as an upcoming operation, deadline or exam) comes closer to fruition. We also have to look at our own perception of the stressor and our tolerance of stress. We each have our own individual way of perceiving and coping with pressure. There is always one person among us who looks forward to tests and exams, and one person who dreads it to the point of becoming ill.

The way in which we cope will determine the short term and long term effects of stress. Some people who have healthy ways of coping; who have a more positive, optimistic view of life, and who take care of themselves physically, may feel less effects of stress and are generally better able to adapt to overall stress factors. Studies prove that having a support system in place is one of the most beneficial aspects to managing stress. If you don't have a supportive friend or confidante, then

I urge you to seek the help of a professional to help you through taxing times.

Speaking with someone who is supportive of your individual experience is beneficial, not only for being able to 'get something off your chest', but also to provide another perspective so you can fully understand your options and make informed decisions. Many of us like to have a second opinion or have help brainstorming ideas. We, as human beings, fare better knowing that we are making decisions based on the 'norm' or standard. Even if we want to be different from others in the way we handle stressors, or in the way we base our decisions, we continue to solicit others opinions and advice because it makes us feel better. We gauge our stress levels by how others would deal with the same stressor.

Our conditioning comes about in part by our environment and childhood role models. If a child grows up with a parent who is a hypochondriac, for example, that child may perceive illness as a great source of stress and may actually take on some of the characteristics of an illness. Or may be unable to protect them self from illness. Another child may grow up with a caregiver who is a chronic worrier or is overly protective. The child then does not fully form an attachment with his or her own ability to self protect or see options to overcome worry and fear. Of course this does not happen in all cases, but the protective factors that combat stress may be weakened. This is related to our perceptions and belief systems, which we now know can be changed and expanded in order for us have the ability to view other options.

It is important for us to be aware of any given stressor so that we can view it objectively and align ourselves with options. Being mindful and practicing mindful meditation can help greatly with this. Whenever we can stay in the present moment and view a stressor as detached from emotion and ego, we can better be able to categorize what is happening and how to best deal with it. When we allow stress to take over our minds, our options and perception of how to deal with and handle the stressor become skewed and overshadowed by our emotions.

There is what we counsellors call an 'internal' or 'external' locus of control. This is to say that we individually view stressors, as well as other behaviours, to be inside of our control or being outside of our control.

People who have an internal locus of control will view events as something that they have the ability to handle, or change within themselves. They take responsibility for their thoughts, emotions, and actions. They see themselves as being in charge of their own behaviours and the outcomes that they desire.

Individuals who view their stressors and behaviours as being outside of their control are said to have external locus of control. These people usually perceive behaviours, stressors or events as being outside of their control. They believe their control lies with someone else. They believe other people have the ability to control their stressors, but not themselves. These individuals do not typically take responsibility for their own ability to handle or change a stressful situation. They look to others to solve problems and they feel that they don't have the power to change things for themselves.

Needless to say, people who typically have an internal locus of control are able to better adapt to and find options within themselves to decrease and deal with stressful situations in their life. The effects of stress do not impact their physical or psychological health to the same degree that people who have an external locus of control do. The good news is that we can change the locus of control that we have now. We can adopt a mindset of taking personal responsibility for how we perceive our lives and the people and events that are in it, as well as what we can do about them.

Understand that you cannot change other people, but you can change the way in which their negative behaviours impact you. You can take responsibility for how others treat you. You can speak up and let others know when you feel disrespected by them and how you would like to be treated. If another person disrespects you, you are in charge of how you respond to him or her and you decide what part that the individual will play in your life. Refusing to engage with a person who continually stresses you out is a good way to get the point across that you are not going to enable that person to treat you in the same way that he or she has in the past. We all need to have more communication with people whose behaviours don't sit well with us. You don't need to be argumentative or disrespectful with them, but you do need to hold true to, and honour, yourself.

If you feel you are unable to stand up to certain people, such as your boss, then recognize that this person plays no role in your personal life. Leave this person at work.

I am certainly aware that when others feel a need to act out negatively by venting their power and control issues, they are suffering. You can learn how to reframe your perception of this person. Finding compassion for a person who is stressing you out on a daily basis seems ludicrous, but that person is suffering with his or her own negativity and low self worth issues and is trying to get his or her need for power and control met through you. I visualize having full rain gear on and allowing other people's negative behaviours to bounce off me like raindrops. Their negative energy does not penetrate and my self esteem is left fully intact. I do not engage my emotions or ego with a person who demonstrates those qualities because that is exactly what their ego wants. You don't want to enable that person to continue their abuse towards you, but at the same time you are sending a message that you will not engage their ego or allow them to meet their dysfunctional needs through you. In the meantime, if you are dealing with a difficult boss, you may feel a need to form an exit strategy and find a workplace that promotes mutual respect.

Life is way too short to allow the negativity of others to affect your stress levels or peace of mind. But I do understand and recognize that there are times when you feel you have to stay in a place of negativity or high stress for the time being. It is helpful to recognize for yourself that this is a temporary situation and that you are working towards a goal of peace and tranquility. Because stress is also a state of mind, it is possible to find peace and alleviate stress even in a demanding environment.

Reframing a negative or stressful situation can help immensely in bringing about change for yourself. This strategy allows you to expand the options you have. When we choose to think and interpret a situation, event or person as stressful, we should remember that we can choose another way of interpreting that same situation, event or person. When I speak with someone who is negative and choosing to create stress, I will first start by talking to them about their influence. I see that person, for example, as suffering with negativity because in reality, someone who chooses to be negative is suffering and disconnecting with their higher source. They shut off their connection with the universe (or higher power) and in effect stop the good from coming into their life.

Knowing about the gifts that our higher source can bring us, I can't help but feel pity for people who miss out on such wonders. When I feel that a person is suffering I don't feel anger, but rather empathy and sympathy for their plight. This sets up a whole different dynamic for me. When I do this, that person no longer has the power over me to create stress in my life.

I don't compare people to animals, for surely we are more evolved. But for the purpose of understanding and clarity, I will use animals for this example. If you see a wounded animal, you want to help it even if the animal is trying to protect itself by being aggressive towards you. We tend to understand why the animal is in protection mode and we try our best to help anyway. In essence, people tend to act this way to one another as well. We now recognize that the 'bully' is just someone who suffers from low self esteem, power and control issues and quite possibly abuse. The person who continually brags and is arrogant suffers from a feeling of ineptness. Each of these types of people is trying pitifully to gain some semblance of control over their own lives by attempting to make others feel bad.

A simple statement in a conversational, but assertive tone, such as, "please don't speak to me in that way" along with eye contact, goes a long way in letting people know that you are not open to negotiation when it comes to how they can treat you. If they continue to speak to you in that way, reinforce your previous statement. You may also choose to walk away at that point and refuse to engage that person. He or she will get the message.

There is little room for misunderstanding of what you are saying. Do not harbour ill will towards that person. Instead, release it to the universe, or your higher power, and move on. Don't worry; you will not melt into a puddle on the ground. You have not been rude or aggressive; you have been assertive.

It helps to know that we do choose how we feel, think and act about any given situation, event or person. You need to have balance in every aspect of your life. Yes, I do mean all areas of your life. If you think that you can't have balance due to high job stress or family demands, it is because you have established a pattern of behaviour over time that has dictated a lack of balance. Thankfully, more employers are beginning to recognize the need for balance in the workforce. More companies are giving people 'family time' as well as sick time. More people are being able to work from home at times as well. More and more employers are recognizing that there is actually increased productivity from their employees when balance is given priority.

Part of finding balance in order to minimize stress is to become mindful in everything you do. Be present with each task and you will become more efficient and able to think of different ways to tackle even the most challenging of projects (or people). Studies are now proving that multi-tasking is not as effective at getting more done as focusing on one job at a time. You actually save time and effort this way! You also keep your stress levels lower. And remember, you always have choices.

Above all, I urge you to incorporate some sort of meditation into your daily practice. Meditating is free, portable and readily available. It is one of the best things that you can do for yourself to combat stress and anxiety, as well as a host of other negative issues. Meditation will immediately slow down and rid your mind of all the 'chatter' that goes on in your head. When you quiet the chatter, you are then in a position to bring about a connection with your higher power and resolutions become available to you because you are then able to focus in on the issue. I will go into greater detail about meditation in an upcoming chapter.

If you choose not to meditate, try yoga or tai chi (there are many options), or whatever helps to ground you. I always ask people to focus in on what is going on in their immediate environment, at the very moment they feel stressed or anxious. Are you safe at this moment? Identify what is in your immediate environment, where you are, who is there and what is happening. This helps to ground you in the here and now. Being in the moment will not allow stress or anxiety to take hold. It is your immediate reality and not what you are thinking about.

Anxiety comes from forward thinking, so if you bring your thoughts back into the immediate moment you will rid yourself of the apprehension. It only takes a few moments to calm the mind chatter and you will see positive results immediately!

This grounding technique also works for past thinking. Thinking in the past can produce guilt and shame and can create immense stress and anxiety. The grounding technique I've described above works for past thinking as well. I have also used this technique for clients who have faced traumatic events and have regressed into another mental state. Living in the here and now is the best way to go. You can plan for the future and think about the past but do it mindfully and your stressors will stay to a minimum. After all, you are only actually living at this moment!

CHAPTER 6

CHANGING NEGATIVE BEHAVIOURS

Of all that I wish to convey in this book, I ultimately want you, the reader, to find the ability to change your own negative behaviours; however those behaviours may look to you. We all come with our own unique set of demeanours and issues, so what one person perceives as negative may not be perceived the same by another. Because of this, I will try and generalize my suggestions for overcoming negative behaviours.

I think that most, if not all; negative issues can be overcome with a positive mindset. There is little room for negativity in a positive outlook. We are all human beings and we live in a society that presents us with many negative situations. There are many times when we react in a negative way; whether it is a thought, emotion or action. The first thing I will suggest is for you to give yourself permission to stumble once in a while, without being negative towards yourself.

As I started out on my path to self discovery, I spoke with my Monk about the fact that I was frustrated in my inability to transform myself as quickly as I would have liked. My Monk responded by telling me that it's okay to stumble on my path to enlightenment because after all, I was an ordinary human being. This meant that I am on my path to enlightenment but I am still living in this human body in this human world. And in this human world, no one is perfect. At the same time, do not use this fact as a crutch and engage in negative behaviours as routine.

Any change that is significant takes time and effort. You must be mindful of what you are doing and what outcome you would like to achieve. There are mind steps we go through in our pursuit for change and they are similar to Kubler-Ross' Stages of Grief. The stages this chapter will cover can use for any change you are experiencing or any decisions you need to make.

I will be referring to the **Stages of Change**, which was clearly mapped out by James Prochaska, PH.D, John Norcross, PH.D and Carlo Diclemente PH.D in the book 'Changing for Good' and is referred to as the **Transtheoretical Model of Change**. I am going to explain these stages to you so that you can recognize and understand which stage of change you are in and what you need to do to move on in your transformation process. The Stages of Change are universal, especially when undergoing a significant behavioural modification (remember that behaviours encompass anything you say, think or do).

As humans, we are not prone to experience change in a clean cut linear way. It is more like a spiral of change; we go around and around and in and out of stages as we learn different behaviours and become comfortable with them. I've stated before that we choose to live in a way that is comfortable for us even if it dysfunctional, because it is what we know; it's conditioned. At some point, we also figure out (hopefully) that our current dysfunctional behaviour is not working for us or getting us the results that we desire.

In other instances, we change our behaviour because we are compelled to by others, whether it's a significant person in our lives or if it is mandated by a court system, due to drug use, etc. If a person is attempting to change because of someone else's wishes, they are at high risk for failure. The new behaviour may be sustained for a period of time, but the mindset is not connected to the change and can therefore revert back to dysfunctional behaviour quite easily. We need to engage our mental, emotional, physical and spiritual characteristics to effect sustained change.

It starts with some inkling of awareness that something is not working right, or we want something more out of our lives. Whether it's a negative behaviour you're trying to banish or some personality shortfall you would like to change but don't know how to; there is some feeling, thought or emotion that generally spurs us onto delve deeper and discover what it is we want to change.

Don't disregard the feedback from others when trying to change your negative behaviour. Most people will not give you unsolicited feedback, except maybe close friends or family, so ask for feedback about yourself from those that you think will be honest and open. If you do ask for feedback about yourself, be prepared to be open to receiving it. Look at the constructive criticism as a great chance to grow as a human being. It does not help if everyone in your world only gives you positive responses because you don't get the chance to hear what needs tweaking or changing in your life. Sometimes we need to hear unpleasant things about ourselves in order to provide us with personal growth. So perceive this feedback as a positive experience and a chance to grow as a divine human being.

Stage 1: Precontemplation

Precontemplation is just what is sounds like. You are not contemplating change but have some inkling that something is not feeling right for you. You can't necessarily put your finger on it and are not necessarily looking for change at this time. In this stage, you may be receiving feedback or criticism around a particular behaviour that you possess. You may hear things like "you don't listen to me when I'm speaking to you", "you're not following through with your ideas", "you can be really harsh with people", and etc. Depending where you get it from, you may have conditioned yourself to 'turn off' when you hear this feedback.

In this stage you may start to become mindful around your particular behaviours and do what I call 'window shopping'. This is to say that you may start to hear things that you previously tuned out, and an 'aha' moment will happen. Something will start to resonate from within to your conscious mind. You may become aware as you continue to receive negative feedback from others; whether it is a statement, action or non-action behaviour (cold shoulder or avoidance) from others. You may start to gather information to see what resonates with you. You may start to 'hear' information that you previously tuned out subconsciously. Some information or behaviour that you may not normally be interested in suddenly becomes interesting or informative. Some shift in consciousness will take over and you will behave differently towards it. Like window shopping, you are just looking, trying things out but are not yet ready to buy (or in this case buy into the new behaviour).

You may test the water, so to speak, like dipping your toe into a pool to test the water temperature. The information that you hear or gather will be generic and generalized in nature. It may be difficult to come to the realization that you need to change behaviour. We tend to go to the place of "If I have to change this about me, then there must be something wrong with me". This type of thinking can keep you from connecting to your higher source. I urge you not to get caught up in this egoic thinking. You have only one life in your body and it is short, so get past the ego and do this for yourself. As a divine human being, you deserve to live the best life you can and you deserve to be joyful and abundant.

Stage 2: Contemplation

In this stage, you are thinking on a conscious level and weighing your options. You recognize that something is not working well in your life and are likely going through 'the great debate' in your mind, looking for information about your options. This is the stage where you may solicit feedback from others, look more specifically for information about the behaviour in question and brainstorm ideas to change. You will be looking at decision making in this stage.

One tool I use with people who are in this stage of change is called the 'Decisional Matrix Scale'. This stage helps you map out the 'Pros' and 'Cons' of the change in question. It helps you to better understand the best direction to take. Essentially, you will look at the short and long term effects of changing the behaviour versus keeping the behaviour. It looks like this:

I encourage you to create a separate decisional matrix for each change or decision that you need to make. This is a great tool to use when you need to make any major decision as well. When you are stuck in your thinking, the decisional matrix will help you to get all the pros and cons out of your head and onto paper. This way you can clear the mind clutter and make a decision based on clarity of thinking rather than just intellect or emotions.

Simply write out a word or phrase that comes into your mind for the pro or con section, including short and long term goals. Then go through the list and weigh how much each 'pro' and 'con' will affect you mentally, physically, emotionally and spiritually. How significant is each 'pro' and 'con'? You should also include the consequences of the change for yourself and significant others, as well as the reactions to this change from yourself and significant others. This is important because the decisions you make will not only impact you but those you care about. This will help you to make an informed decision that will be best for you. When you make a decisional matrix, a picture will emerge that will help you to see things more clearly, give you increased confidence in yourself and your decisions, and help you to visualize your outcome more positively.

The decisional matrix is a useful tool and can clarify behaviours and decisions, but I will ask that you seek the help of a professional with experience in behavioural change if you are uncertain about any aspects of completing this yourself. It may also be helpful to get input from others if you are having difficulty coming up with any 'pros' or 'cons', or if some of your 'conditioned responses' are getting in the way of obtaining positive

Cheryl Hitchcock

growth. But remember that this is for you and any other input should be objective.

You should have a clearer understanding of what you need to do, or which direction you need to proceed in when you have the visual in front of you. You can then forge ahead with confidence! There will be some preparation needed before you change the behaviour and have real sustained change, which brings me to the next stage of change.

Contemplation Stage
Decisional Matrix

Short Term   Long Term

Pros:	Cons:	Pros:	Cons:
Consequences To Self:	Consequences To Others:	Reactions From You:	Reactions From Others:

Stage 3: Preparation (or Determination)

The preparation stage of change can be one of the most significant stages that you go through in your quest for positive change, or change of any kind. In the preparation stage, you are literally preparing your mind, body and spirit for modification. This stage has the most potential for fear when letting go of old, familiar and sometimes dysfunctional behaviours. The old adage "better the devil you know" comes into play. You may decide to exit at this stage or go back to a previous stage until "the time is right" to proceed again.

This stage requires the physical, mental and spiritual work required to ensure change is effective. That means different things for different people but fear issues seem to stay constant. I urge you to let go of your subconscious need for control and keep your eyes and your energy directed towards the ultimate goal. This is the stage where you may need to seek guidance from a professional because of the lack of direction on how to proceed, or at least for a push through the feelings that come up; whether they are feelings of fear, lack, overwhelm, sadness, frustration, criticism by others or lack of support in general. This stage may feel lonely at times and you may question whether it is worth it or not.

In order to move ahead, you need to compile the information you require to make an informed decision about what you want to change and how to make it come into effect. I recommend putting together a goal map. A goal map involves writing out your vision for change. It may be easier to start from the end goal and work backwards. The following are the steps and timelines you must take to ensure you stay on track:

- List your ultimate goal

- Make a list of short term and long term goals that should be met to reach the ultimate objective.

- Break down the lists into long term goals and immediate goals (less than one week)List goals that you want to meet within six weeks

- List goals that you want to meet within three months

- List goals that you want to meet in six months and then one year.

- Make a list of goals that you want to meet in the second, third and up to fifth year.

- You can break these goals down to short and long term goals with the coming of each new year.

With the short and long term goals listed, you also need to work on the individual steps involved in achieving each one. The steps in the long term goals do not need to be too detailed but should include things you need to keep your eye on, such as places you can hold workshops, or a space for your new business, etc.

Once you've set out your goals, you can elicit help from others to get the steps done in order to reach them. From the immediate goals, from the first 24 hours to the end of the first week, you should write 'to do' lists. With each objective, you must break down when you are going to complete the task, which will help you and how you are going to achieve this. It may sound like a lot of work but believe me, a little work up front will make it simple for you to stay on track and achieve the goals you set out for yourself in a clear, concise manner that will keep the stress to a minimum. Your chances of successfully achieving your goals will be increased significantly, you will feel more positive about the change, and your fear and overwhelming feelings will be kept at bay. This will become your roadmap to success. Your plan will be organized and in writing so that you can be clear to focus on each step of the success ladder, rather than feeling anxious about all of the tasks that you need to complete (which is usually responsible for people exiting the change process and not succeeding with their goals). So why not eliminate the roadblocks right up front?

The above process is a natural one for your mind and the information is stored in your brain. The difference is that if you keep this information in your mind, it becomes jumbled and unclear, thus leading to anxiety and a lack of clear direction. You will undoubtedly miss a few key steps along the way and it will therefore take you longer and with less efficiency to achieve your goals. You are also more prone to giving up. With the goal matrix, you don't have to keep thinking about what you have to do in order to stop yourself from forgetting, it's all written down in front of you in black and white and you simply need to consult it for the next step. It couldn't be easier. The challenge comes from resisting the urge to 'just do what seems easier right now'.

This really is an easy process that will help you better visualize your ideas, dreams and goals and become excited about the change process. You should use this for every ambition that you want to achieve. I've given you an example of what a plan looks like but tailor it to your own goals and creativity.

Cheryl Hitchcock

1.1 Goal Matrix

Goal: Start my own business

Short term Goals:

Today:

Work on picking out a name for the business and writing out a vision for my business.

Who will complete this task: I will complete this task with input from my children and partner.

I will meditate and give thanks and gratitude for all that I have in my life. I will do this *twice per day, every day.*

I will focus positive energy on all my tasks and send out loving kindness to my fellow human beings *every day.*

This week:

I will look into tax laws, information and criteria for owning a sole proprietor business in my province/state.

I will check out online businesses that are similar to mine and glean useful information for marketing my business, pricing information, choosing target markets, determining what information I should include on my website, creating brochures, etc.

My friend Marsha will help me with this on Tuesday. I will work on this for 2 hours each day as well.

Next two weeks:

I will have finished choosing a name for my business and will have written out my vision statement.

I will work on the information I need to provide about me and my business (for future brochures, cards, website, etc.) My friend Norman will help me with this on Wed and Friday of next week.

I will register my business with the government.

I will start looking for suppliers, virtual assistants, space, wholesalers, and web designers.

My friends Norman, Marsha and Jill will also help with this on Wednesday.

Next month:

I will have a list of suppliers, virtual assistants, available space, wholesalers, web designers, etc. and start narrowing down help and checking them out via the web and references. *Jill will help me with this.*

I will write out a business plan with the help of my partner.

I will look into financial costs and determine the amount of loans if any that I will need.

I will access the government website of available money for grants, business loans, etc.

I will speak to my bank manager as well as other banks to find out who has the best deal for small businesses (interest rates, loans, credit, and monthly fees).

I will look for and attend free workshops about starting a small business. My partner and friends will keep their eyes open for these. I will also access information on the internet.

Three months:

I will have completed my business plan. I will take two weeks to prepare this in month two.

I will choose a bank to help with my business needs.

I will choose my team (accountant, bookkeeper, lawyer, and staff).

I will access money from other avenues for grants, loans, from the government website. Send in prepared package with business plan before individual cut off dates. I will follow up with them one to two weeks later by phone.

I will have cards and brochures printed with my information, using my chosen colours, format, and chosen stock, font and pictures.

I will speak with suppliers, wholesalers and other business contacts that I have prepared from a short list of people I have spoken with and determine who I will be going with.

My friend Marsha will help me with this if I need her.

Six months:

Month four - Any required funds will be in place for materials, space, overhead costs.

Month four and five - Materials and space will be picked out.

Month five - Materials and space will be paid for.

Month five - Will move materials into space.

Month five and six - I will make sure marketing and promotion is up and running. Virtual Assistant will help me with this. My partner and child will help with distribution of written material to homes and offices.

End of month six - Move in to new space and have grand opening.

Six months to One year:

Make sure bookkeeper and accountant are up to date and informed of progress.

Monitor online website re: marketing and promotions, events, etc. *My Virtual Assistant will do this.*

Make sure supplies are stocked and merchandise, etc. is available. I will continue to keep up to date with new suppliers, etc.

Make sure business plan is being adhered to. Look for other avenues of funding.

Create new lines and streams of income. *My partner and friend Norman will help with this.*

Give generous donation to the food bank or other charity.

<u>Long Term Goals:</u>

Two to Three Years

 Be able to let go of any other jobs and do this one full time with the income that exceeds $60,000.00+ per year aside from operating costs.

Write a book about my business and how I can help other Small Business Owners.

Hold annual charity event and give back generously.

Hire a personal assistant.

Determine if space and websites need to be updated. My virtual assistant and personal assistant will help with this.

Create or join like- minded individuals for mastermind or networking group.

Do TV and other media promotions.

Drive business nationally and/or internationally. Lawyer, accountant, and assistants will help with this.

Hire more staff if necessary.

Conduct workshops and seminars about my business.

CONGRATULATIONS! You are now able to give up any other jobs because you've made it!

By the way, this took me about 45 minutes to produce. If you are unsure of what you need to do, ask for help, consult the web, or call a professional. This is a sample of a goal map; the timelines can be much more strict, right down to a daily agenda. This sample will get you started and, as you tick off the steps that you have taken, you will feel a great sense of accomplishment, and excitement at seeing your dreams take flight and your goals realized. Remember that as you go through the actual process, you may need to edit or add steps as they arise, so don't forget to write them on your goal map.

This is only one type of map but you should use a goal map for any change, whether it's starting a new business or direction in your life or changing a bad habit or negative behaviour. .

ACTION STAGE

Now that you have your goal map set out and you are clear about what you need to do to take action around, do it! In the action stage, you simply start implementing what you have written down. In the preparation stage you have an agenda and steps you need to take. Whatever yours looks like, start doing it.

As you begin to take action you begin to see results. This stage may require you to step outside of your comfort zone and learn different things, challenge your belief systems about what you are capable of doing, and change the way in which you see the world. Taking action is required for any change to take place. It is essential for you to view this in a positive light rather than with fear as your guide. Your mindset will inform your outcome, so you need to remain positive in the presence of fear, see the fear for what it is; a manifestation of the ego to prevent you from connecting to your higher source.

There will be some deep soul searching involved here in order to make sure you have aligned your goals with your internal higher source. Giving things up that are on a lower spiritual level (or non-spiritual level) may be difficult at first, but deeper understanding of what your life path is and how you can achieve that, is something that sits outside your comfort zone and will therefore take a certain amount of introspection. It may seem difficult to give up something that you've done in order to gain great strides in your life. But the Universe is, and always will, give you what you want and need. It is our own fear of release that keeps us stuck and unable to achieve greatness. This may be especially difficult if it means releasing people in our lives that are non-supportive and negative.

For example, if you are starting your own business and are used to drinking with buddies after work every night, you may have to change your routine in order for you to focus on building your new business. If in turn your buddies are negative towards your new found goals, they may become negative and unsupportive towards what you are doing. You may start to attract like-minded people who will enhance your business, but if you are unwilling to change your former lifestyle, you may find that the business is failing. This does not mean that you have to give up your buddies entirely, but as you start to succeed and negativity continues to bring you down, you have serious decisions to make. Remember that you are the only one who walks your path in life and you are responsible for the changes you make.

Surround yourself with all that will enhance your life and you will find that you gain even more from the Universe than you could imagine. The fear of change will become a welcome companion instead. You need to be clear about what it is that you want and what you are willing to change to make gains in your life. If you are not sure what seems to keep you from fulfilling your goals, even though you've made a detailed map of what they are, that's when you need to go inside yourself and take a good, honest look at what's holding you back. You will find the answers if you have the courage to go deep within yourself to find what's lacking.

Calm the chatter that goes on in your mind and meditate. The answers to all of your questions, doubts and fears will emerge when the mind is still. This is when you find the direction and action that you need to take.

Are you doubtful about your abilities to change? Do you have deep beliefs about success and wealth that keep you from achieving it? Do you doubt your greatness? These are the deep, meaningful and egoic messages that prevent you from aligning with your higher source and receiving the greatness that you were meant to have. Don't send these messages deeper into your subconscious and try to forget about them because these subconscious messages will ultimately drive the outcomes you experience.

I have often heard from clients that meditation is hard for them to do. I practice a few different forms of meditation but the Buddhist Vipissana meditation seems to be the more difficult form to master. This is the practice of clearing your mind of all thoughts and directing your focus towards your breath. I was told by my Monk that it is the quality of meditation not the quantity that is best. So even if you can only clear your mind at first for a minute or so, that is great. With practice, you will be able to spend more time in this state, and you will start to feel more grounded and peaceful.

In Vipissana meditation, I am able to easily get in touch with the higher source of my energy. This state is where I am able to manifest and enhance my greatness. As always, once you start to manifest your own greatness you also are able to send out the energy that helps others to manifest their greatness.

As you go through the action stage of change you may find challenges around what you need to do to affect change. What helps is increasing your awareness of what the challenge is and what you know you can and cannot do. If you are uncertain, calm your mind to receive the help from the Universe. You may have the help that you need right in front of you, but if you are unaware or preoccupied with the egoic mind then you may not see the help or opportunity you need. Be conscious and aware of what is happening around you and keep your mind open to different ways that the help can come to you. If you only think that you can receive the help in one way, your mind is closed to the many other opportunities that you have heading your way. Keep your mind open, don't decide how and when your opportunities will arrive, and increase your awareness about what it is that you need. I think of this as a sort of 'treasure hunt'. When I need something to change I put out my request to the Universe and then I keep my eyes and ears open to receive what the Universe is providing for me.

Remember to take action, be proactive and become aware of what you need to do. Look inside yourself to see what internal changes need to be done and take action there as well. Stop the excessive mind chatter and get in touch with your higher source to help banish any negativity from inside you and from outside sources. Be willing to step outside your comfort zone and trust that you will be safe in doing so. You can't keep doing the same, comfortable things and expect different results! Align your thoughts, emotions and actions and take pride in the incredible results that *you* have created.

Maintenance Stage

The maintenance Stage of Change also requires action. Now that you have had your honeymoon period of change, you need to sustain the modifications for life, not just for a few months, or years. This stage is probably as difficult, if not more, than the Action stage. You are riding the 'high' of seeing positive results and being able to manifest the change you needed, but how are you going to sustain it?

My hope is that you have changed your mindset and lifestyle enough to help you through the challenges of maintaining this positive change. There is always the Ego that needs looking out for and looking after. The old ways of behaving may be easier than sustaining new change and sometimes we just don't have the energy to keep it up.

You need to avoid any self talk and action that can sabotage your new life. Be prepared to protect the change that you have worked so diligently for, and continue to connect to your higher source for positive energy. As you become more connected with your life source, you will see more and more profound change. Connecting to and using your energy source will always help you grow and sustain change. . Your Ego may want to continually 'trick' you into thinking that you can go back to what you were doing, thinking or feeling before you changed, but don't get caught up in this. Our minds (and Ego) can only think so big or small, but the Universe can provide us with so much more than we can ever imagine...

You may end up 'doing battle' in your head when the 'newness' wears off your positive transformation. Again, this is the ego attempting to sabotage you. This is the stage that can cause people to derail after undergoing change. I have seen people write another letter to their old habits or behaviours at this stage, saying good-bye forever and welcoming their new life. Try this or whatever helps you to stay the course. You may find yourself getting into a place where you feel overwhelming temptations or overconfidence with your change. Be aware of these as this can sabotage your efforts.

I also suggest finding support groups or a mentor to help you at this stage. Someone who can help you sustain the changes you have made. This draws like-minded people to you and can expand and enhance your life. Networking to continually move to more positive awareness and change is also constructive. Always, when making any kind of change, make sure that what you are taking away (a negative behaviour) is replaced with something that is meaningful (positive) to you. This will help to sustain and maintain the change. For example, if you quit smoking, you should replace the cigarette with something that is meaningful to you. One way is to use your cigarette money for something that you have wanted, either by spending small amounts more frequently, or saving for something big that you couldn't previously afford. You decide what is meaningful to you.

You must also continue to increase your awareness of, not only yourself, but everything that is going on in your world. As you increase your understanding of yourself, you can prevent negative thoughts, emotions or actions and head them off before they do any damage if they try and re-emerge.

When behavioural change is maintained, it does become ingrained, becoming the 'norm', and it does get easier with time. This is the '***termination***' stage of change. The new behaviour is now a sustained behaviour and is no longer in the change cycle. Congratulations! You can now move on to bigger and better change. I decided not to give this its own section because it seems to be fairly self-explanatory.

I think back to some of the behaviours I displayed as a young woman and I could not fathom having those behaviours in my life now. They seem so foreign to me now. I have long since banished any negative thoughts and emotions that may have caused guilt or shame. They are all steps in my life that have helped me learn what I want, and don't want in my life, and have lead me to the true path that I am on. When I think of the long periods of time I lacked direction and seemed to be going around in circles, I am thankful that I was determined and aware enough to know that there was something better waiting for me. Through my awareness, the Universe has provided me with many wonderful experiences that have guided me to where I am today.

Relapse

I won't spend too much time or energy on this section because I think most people who have heard anything about behavioural change are somewhat aware of this. It is important to know about relapse but it does need some description for educational purposes.

Relapse, lapse and prolapse are the stages of change that occur when we are on our path to sustained change. I am going to lump them together here for the purpose of explaining how this fits into the process of change, but not to build it up to the point of sabotaging your change.

Most of you will hear of relapse as a switch back to the 'old' behaviours that you are trying to modify. Some belief systems out there dictate that if you have only one lapse back to an old behaviour (say having one drink) then you hopelessly failed at your mission. I say hogwash. When you were a baby and you learned to walk, I'll bet you stumbled and failed a couple of times before you mastered the art of walking. This is true of any significant behavioural change. Although with harmful behaviours, I should state that I do not condone relapsing, but I must explain that relapsing is a normal part of the change process. If it sounds like I'm doing some dancing here,

Cheryl Hitchcock

it is because many clients I've worked with who have displayed self harming behaviours (such as major drug or alcohol use, abuse, anger, etc.) have been known to use the relapse stage as a crutch and permission to be able to engage in harmful behaviour. Relapse can be normal and should not be seen as abject failure. It does not need to be seen as a character flaw in the person who is changing. As we try on new behaviours, we will undoubtedly reject some and embrace others. And while this is happening, we come back around to the old ways of being. Make sure to always resume your path when you have encountered a relapse. Make sure to be gentle with yourself and don't play the self saboteur, or beat yourself up over this. It will only feed more negative behaviours and cause more damage to the change process, as well as to the connection with your higher source. Always remember to love yourself; that way you can show and give love to others.

CHAPTER 7

FINDING YOUR SPIRITUAL CENTRE

When I talk about finding your Spiritual Centre, what I mean is finding your essence as a spiritual being; your core energy that directs you to the place you are in now, and your connection to your higher source. This is not necessarily a religious practice, so I am not going to label this one way or another. Whether you consider your higher source to be energy, divine essence, God, Allah, Buddha, the Universe, or anything else, this chapter will not focus on one particular name. It's that spiritual aspect inside all of us that sets us aside from our human behaviours and yet drives us to understand who we are and what we are truly meant to do in this life. When you establish a true connection to your Spiritual Centre, you achieve peace, understanding, and a connection to all life on the planet including: guidance, joy, love and abundance.

When we find our Spiritual Centre, there is no anxiety, doubt, depression, worry, guilt or shame; there is only truth. The source of our Spiritual Centre is within all of us and we all have access to it. It's free, portable, accessible and plentiful. The challenge that some find with accessing the Spiritual Centre is that it takes some practice and diligence, just as anything we learn in life does. We learn our beliefs and religious practices and mould our lives and practices around them. Because of this, we all have the skills necessary to find our Spiritual Centre, as well as the methods to learn to practice spirituality and connect to our higher source.

Connecting to our Spiritual Centre is a kind of paradox. It requires releasing and concentrating at the same time. It may seem to go beyond logic, but at the same time connecting with our Spiritual Centre integrates our daily human activities. It may sound like a lot of work but it's quite a simple process. This process requires you to look inward rather than outside of yourself. In our daily practice, we can use our connection to source when we look outward at the world around us. This may sound like a riddle or a Buddhist exercise on insight, but we all have this ability to connect should we choose to use it. If it is used, the world in which we exist changes, as well as our existence within it.

I am going to attempt to keep this process as simple as I can without taking away from the fundamental core of it. When I was taught by Buddhist Monks how to find my centre and truly connect with pure truth, I couldn't believe how easy it was (I thought that I must be doing something wrong!) but at the same time, I couldn't get over how challenging it can be to stay connected with the source at times. It is truly amazing how conditioned we, as humans, are to always have chatter in our minds at any given time. This was truly much like taming a wild beast for me. It continues to be just as challenging at times, but the good thing is that the wild beasts that are my mental constructs are not as wild or as rampant as they once were. I now have more control over my mental processes than they have over me. I can step away from the ego and see a situation or person truthfully rather than what my ego-based perceptions would want to interpret.

As you begin to master connection with your Spiritual Centre, your true authentic self will emerge. This is not your personality but your inner essence; the divine human being that you are who has the ability to see the truth about your existence; the existence that is devoid of conditioned constructs and that are connected to cognitive thought processes and ego based thinking. It is about seeing and living in the moment, even if that moment requires future thinking or past remembering. It's about moving away from the fuel that keeps the ego mind engaged and seeing things in a pure, detached way. I call it the objective observer; seeing things without being subjective and adding your narrative and emotions to a situation, person, or event.

It may seem difficult to understand what truly living in the moment requires and that our true reality has little to do with our preconceived notions of what is happening at this very moment. We tend to filter how we perceive things. If I ask you what is happening at this very moment, you could say that your life is great, that you have a wonderful partner and love and joy is in your life, but that is not what is required of being in the moment. This may be your current life situation but what I am asking is what is going on at this very moment with you? You in fact are probably reading this statement right now. You may be sitting on a chair or couch and you are in your living room just "being". After all, as Dr. Wayne Dyer once said,

"We are human beings, not human doings or human thinkings".

This very moment is the only reality that we live in. The past is but a memory and the future is not yet here, we only have now. To gain true connection with the higher source, we must live in the now, not in the past or future because that is not reality. We may have to temporarily think in the future or in the past, but there is a huge difference from temporarily thinking to living in the past or future.

When we live in the past or the future, we cease existing in the present and cease to live in real time. We then miss out on what is happening now. Our existence is not real when we are not present. It is a mind construct based on subjective thoughts and emotions. A great example of this is when we project our minds to a future time where we must face something unknown to us. In thinking about the unknown and not knowing the outcome, our egos begin to construct various outcomes that may or may not happen. We then usually go to worst case scenarios if the fear has emotional fuel added to it. We do this regardless of knowing that 99 percent of the time the worst case scenario never comes true. So we waste our reality which is the 'now' and make ourselves worried, sometimes to the point of making ourselves feel sick and anxious about the outcome, or giving up altogether.

Living in the present moment is a necessary part of the process of connecting to the higher source but not the only thing we must do. Therefore, if we live truly in this moment, we cannot experience anxiety, depression, worry or other unsatisfactory emotions. We experience those moments of lack by putting our thoughts into the future or into the past, even if it's only for the next moment or hour. This is the challenge of staying connected to the source. It doesn't mean that you cannot make plans for the hereafter, but living in the past or future is what gets us into unnecessary negative thoughts and conditions. Understanding this and living and functioning in our daily activities may seem impossible but it can be achieved.

As we begin to make future plans, we do have the ability to remain in the present moment. This requires awareness of the here and now and understanding the difference between making a plan for the time to come and living in the future. I can be aware that I am writing a plan and objectively look at the steps I need to take to achieve my goal, without attaching mental constructs and emotions to it. I am aware that I am in my home writing plans on paper or on my computer while not getting caught up in the emotions and thoughts of how to control the outcome; how I think my plan needs to come into fruition, or when all this will happen. Those are the answers that your energy source and Spiritual Centre will bring forth from the Universe. Declare to the Universe and your higher source what the plan or goal is, and you will understand what action is required from you so you can release control and allow the Universe to work 'it's magic'.

There are many practices that can help us find our Spiritual Centre; yoga, meditation, prayer, among others. These are designed to help us clear our heads of egoic thoughts and allow us to focus our attention to a single-focused practice. I will outline the Vipissana meditation as one example of how we can connect to our Spiritual Source and how the essence of this can be translated to any meditative practice that you may choose to do. Vipissana meditation is a Buddhist form of meditation that I learned from the Monks who guided me.

Vipissana meditation requires you to focus solely on your breath as it flows in and out of you. Using the breath to focus on is one of the best ways, but not the only way, to gain single focused concentration. Your breath is always with you, so it's accessible and portable. We all use it, and it allows us to focus our concentration inward to our Spiritual Core, rather than outward to an object that can then take the mind away from inward reflection and start a mental construct about the object that you are looking at.

As you begin your practice of focusing on your breathing, my suggestion is for you to take in two or three cleansing breaths before you start. Breathe in through the nose and out through the mouth. As you are doing this, I recommend concentrating on the point just inside your nostrils where the air hits the hairs in your nose. You can then feel the hairs move as the breath goes in and out. This will help eliminate the mind wanting to wander throughout your whole respiratory system and thus decreasing your single pointed focus.

After you take two or three deep cleansing breaths, continue to breathe through your nose but also exhale through the nose, as you would if you were breathing naturally. Begin to breathe naturally but notice the inhalations and exhalations as a detached observer. Notice them but don't add any labels, narratives, mind constructs or chatter. You may notice that one breath is shallow or one is deeper, but allow the breath to be as it is. Continue to focus on the breath as your mind clears.

If thoughts enter your mind, do not get frustrated and give up, but observe the thought or picture, seeing how is starts and then goes away, simply seeing it come and go in your mind. Take your mind back to your breath and continue to concentrate on it. Intrusions can and do happen, sometimes multiple times during your meditative practice, so don't feel like you are incapable, or give up. As you begin to meditate more you will observe that you are able to enter a deeper state of meditation and your focus and concentration will enhance. You will become more centred and grounded because of this. It is from this place that you are able to access your divine energy and bring it into your everyday existence.

Posture is an important step to take while meditating. Some meditation practices include standing, walking and lying, but they require more concentration and are more advanced. I will talk about sitting meditation for the purposes of beginning the meditative journey. Posture is important because you want to feel energized afterwards as well as calm and peaceful. If you do not practice good posture while meditating you can easily become relaxed and fall asleep, and this is not the purpose of meditation. The purpose is to expand the mind, not put it to sleep. In Vipissana meditation, we sit in lotus or half lotus position. I recognize that some may not be able to get into this position due to physical restraints, so sitting cross legged or with legs extended may be a better alternative. The idea is to have your back straight but not supported by anything, so as not to get too relaxed and fall asleep. It also helps to align your chakras for optimal energy alignment.

You can use a cushion to sit on or a mat. If you use a cushion, it is recommended that the cushion is no more than three inches off the ground when compressed. Your cushion should also only be under your buttocks and not under your legs or your back can be out of alignment and thus cause discomfort. Positioning your cushion in this way will help keep your back straight and your spinal cord and chakras aligned.

Your arms should sit comfortably in your lap with one palm open over the other one, with your forearms resting comfortably on your thighs. This should feel relaxed to you and not an effort. Some will prefer to sit with hands on knees with palms up and your thumb touching your first or second finger creating a circle. This is often the position you see in advertisements of people meditating. The reason for having the fingers or hands joined in a circular way is so the circulation of energy running in and out of you is not broken and released from the body.

I should also mention the posture of the head and neck. In meditation, your spine and chakras should always remain aligned and your head should be erect over the shoulders, not facing down or looking up to the sky. This will help you retain concentration rather than relaxing and dozing off. I recommend closing your eyes during the beginning practices of meditation, but if you choose to have your eyes open, concentrate on a point in front of you that requires you to have your eyes pointed slightly downward but keeping your neck and head straight. This will help with concentration. The reason I suggest that you close your eyes is to reduce the bombardment of stimuli that comes in through our vision. When we see things, we tend to want to label them; our thoughts tend to take over.

One day I told my Monk that, as I became more practiced with my meditation, I seemed to become more distracted. He told me that it was not the quantity of meditation that we do but the quality. A clear mind for only a few minutes can be more beneficial than a long meditation with continual distractions. Think of it like this, when you first learn to drive a car, you are aware of every rule; where your hands are on the steering wheel, what your feet are doing on the peddles and where every car, and pedestrian is in your immediate proximity. But as you become more practiced at driving, most of what you learned becomes ingrained in your head. You begin to drive with one hand on the wheel, listen more to the radio, the rules of the road become loose guidelines. This is because you become comfortable with the driving process and your confidence as a driver increases. As our confidence increases, we tend to 'let down our guard' so to speak. This can happen in meditation practice as well. If you are aware of this, you can become more diligent in your meditation and increase your concentration. You can never be done with meditating, there is always more you can do and discover.

As you deepen your connection with your inner energy and Spiritual Core, you will be able to recreate this state in the other areas of your life, when you are not meditating. Your life begins to take on a more peaceful, calm existence and things don't bother you like they did before. You are able to have more kindness and compassion towards others. You begin to understand the interconnection of all things, and how our energy affects everything and everyone else on this planet. When you become aware of this, you no longer wish to live in the mind constructs that perpetuate negative energy. When negative energy surrounds you, you feel uncomfortable with your life as a whole.

You will continue to face negative energy by virtue of the fact that we do live on this planet with others who may not be able to connect with their Spiritual Centre. You will be able to send your positive energy to those who are not able to bring it to themselves. If we all do this, our suffering on this planet will be significantly diminished.

Finding your Spiritual Centre is not something that we as humans can easily grasp, because it is something that is intangible. We usually think in pictures and the mind is not something that we can easily picture. We can picture our brain and even our body functions, but the mind is something different. We like to think of the mind as thoughts or concepts in an attempt to relate it to something tangible but for many of us, it seems impossible to do.

We can also, after much concentration and inward focus, feel the energy flowing throughout our bodies. But it is more difficult to ask someone to describe their minds. The mind is where thoughts, concepts, beliefs, perceptions and emotions flow from, but it can only be experienced rather than described. The gap from which everything is connected is mind source. This is a Universal Source that allows everything to be interconnected. I would not posit that you get too caught up in how the mind is able to connect to your Spiritual Centre.

The Spiritual Centre can also be a descriptor of the mind. The mind is not a concrete object but is born of the Universal Laws by which we exist, and it exists within every living thing. The mind of a tree lives within the tree. Yes other factors exist to help grow the tree; water, nutrients from soil, etc. but the tree exists and grows, sheds it leaves, and grows again because of its 'mind'. If trees had no minds, they would all grow the same, when given the same conditions. This is the same mind that has salmon swimming great distances each year to breed, regardless of whether they know where they are going or not, or why they need to get there.

Whether you access your mind from a place of academia, religion, spirituality or creativity, you will continue to use the mind in spite of intellect, cognitive function, reasoning, memory function or any other brain activity. I have met many people who lack cognitive functioning, intellect, reasoning or memory performance, who still access the mind to develop themselves in other ways and who are able to access their Spiritual Centre and bring about necessary changes in their lives. They are not marred by the need to rationalize or intellectualize a concept before being able to access their higher consciousness.

The use of the word "consciousness" is one way of describing the mind access, and one which most of us can get our heads wrapped around. From accessing the mind, we can then change the frequency in which our molecules vibrate and change our energy. When we change our energy, we attract the same energy to us. This means that when you emit negative force, you attract lower frequency vibrations. Each and every one of us has the potential to change the energy that we put out, and by putting out positive energy we attract those people and things that are positive as well.

Scientific evidence can now back this theory as humans, especially in the Western world; we have a mindset that if something exists it must be measurable, so that we can think about, and conceptualize it. This may be the reason why more people are recognizing and understanding the power of the mind and positive energy and are starting to use it. Buddhists have known this for over 2500 years and have not felt a need to prove it scientifically.

I remember when I first entered a Buddhist Temple. I was a little wary of what I might be expected to adhere to and if I would have to give up pieces of who I was in order to benefit from the Buddhist teachings. I stated my concerns to my Monk and his reply was "just come and see for yourself". What he further explained is that the Buddhist teachings do not stem from elements outside of you, but rather are cultivated by you and for you. When you learn to connect all that you learn in your mind, you will see the results for yourself, and in all aspects of your life. Buddhism is not something that the Monks dictate or something you must follow or face repercussions. But it is rather teachings to help cultivate your highest levels of consciousness so you can change your own experiences and access an existence here on earth that transcends everyday experiences and perceptions. When you are able to access this, your energy changes in a positive way and you are able to send this out to others. Not surprisingly, the scientific evidence states exactly that. In every part of our physiology and psychology, there are significant benefits to meditation.

I will only caution those who are actively and clinically psychotic to take care with meditation. When someone is experiencing delusions and/or hallucinations actively, focusing on the mind can actually increase them and the person's psychosis level can increase. When the person is free from hallucinations or delusions, the practice of meditation becomes more beneficial.

Our minds are powerful entities and this great power provides us with the ability to live an enlightened existence, not only for ourselves, but for everyone else. This chapter is only the beginning to accessing and living to your highest potential. There are other methods we can use to enhance our existence here on earth and I would like to write another book outlining different ways to enhance our experiences, but for now, this book is a

great start. We are all unique and so are the strategies
we use in our meditation practice.

CHAPTER 8

GIVING BACK

Now that you have worked so diligently at making positive change in your life, it's time to start returning the favour. The Universal Law of reciprocity, or as the Buddhists call, Karma, simply means that there is always a 'cause and effect'; consequences of behaviour, giving back more of the abundance that you receive. Some call this 'tithing' but whatever your perception, it means the same thing. When you receive goodness, you should always pass on the same in kind. From reading this book, my hope is that you have some understanding of the way in which you're energy works, and that because of this, you will receive more of what you put out.

The act of tithing, or giving back, is about the energy exchange you release to the Universal Source. When you release positive energy, you receive positive energy. Giving back is an action that you take to ensure positive energy is released and returned to you. You cannot keep taking and expect that you will receive abundance in an unlimited way. You can amp up the reciprocity by giving back - of yourself, your time or financially. Regardless of how you do it, you should always be thinking about ways in which to be altruistic.

It is important to note that you should not expect to receive anything for what you give. Hopefully, you will appreciate the knowledge you gain from the very act of giving. Doing a kind act only to expect something in return nullifies it and you will therefore find kindness won't be returned to you. The intention behind the act will inform the Law of Reciprocity; if you only perform an act of kindness with the proviso that you will gain something for yourself, then you will not gain. If you perform an act of kindness knowing that you are contributing to the greater good, then you will gain from that knowledge, and positive energy will come back to you. As this positive energy comes back to you, it may be in the form of something that will help you continue on your divine path. Be open to receiving from the Universe and keep your eyes open for the good. It may come to you in ways that you would not normally think of. I compare this to a treasure hunt of good intentions and positive flow that enables you to manifest more of what you need.

Some people have said to me that they are doing good acts but are not receiving the outcomes they had hoped. I would ask what the intention behind their act of kindness was. If what they really wanted to achieve is solely for them they are off track. You really need to look at the intention behind the act. We do not control the 'how' and 'when' of our desired outcomes, we can only release our intentions to the Universe and then connect to the Spiritual Source. We then take action if needed, and wait for the results. The difference between giving back and putting out positive energy is greed. Knowing that you are only doing something to benefit yourself means you do not care about what you are giving back to others. This puts you at odds with what you can truly achieve. There is negative intent behind the act and the intent is what you are truly putting out, so you will therefore receive more negativity or greed.

You can try to fool others, and you can also fool yourself when it comes to your true intentions, but you cannot fool the Universe. That spiritual energy source works out of the depths of the subconscious and will align with that source. Not your conscious, thinking, perceiving world. You may have heard the saying "you can't fool Mother Nature"; well you can't fool the Universe either.

Some say that you should give 10 percent or more to the object of your enlightenment; whether it is your Church, a mentor, a spiritual guide, or whoever brings you knowledge and understanding of your higher self. That is great if you choose to and have the funds to do this. Many people do not. You can give back in other ways. You can give of yourself and do good works for others by volunteering your time or a particular skill set. You can give back by being kind and sending out positive energy and loving thoughts to everyone and everything.

As you begin to truly give back in an authentic, generous and kind way, you will be blessed with insight to the good that the Universe has to offer, including the power to change your existence as well as the existence of others. When one of us is affected in a good way, we all benefit. Give what you can, whenever you can, and don't put limitations towards what and when you can give back. Become excited about giving back, knowing that you are powerful and that you are bringing about the manifestation of good for others as well as for you.

I would like for you to do an exercise. Write down ways in which you can give back. Think about the act of giving back and what it truly means to you. If you write something down and it does not resonate in a positive way with you, then give that some thought. What are your perceptions and beliefs around that particular subject matter? Is this particular act resonating negatively due to ego attachment?

I would like you to go out and give the particular act that is resonating negatively with you a try, but this time remain detached emotionally from the act, and become the objective observer. Does this resonate differently with you now? Continue this practice and you will discover that some 'unmanageable' acts of giving back may now seem quite different.

The act of giving back is as old as history itself. The Bible shows many examples of giving back. In Buddhism it is essential to the process of enlightenment. In this modern age we tend to forget to give back and our focus lies in what we can get for ourselves. It's no wonder, then, why we can feel so disconnected from each other. The 'mine' mindset prevails and we shut each other out. Make no mistake about it, people have always prospered, but for those who have not had the insight to give back, the fall from grace can be painful, and everyone suffers for it.

In our age of technology, we see kids isolating themselves as they socialize via the computer. I am not blaming parents for this; however we need to look at the social aspects of this phenomenon. The technology age has provided us with unprecedented access to a whole new world. It is responsible for a great many things that are positive. We are able to connect to others at great distances and are therefore able to open our minds to many aspects of life that we might not otherwise had access to. But in doing so something else had to be put on the back burner, so to speak. Our time spent with our families and interacting in our own backyards, has become limited. Our society has become increasingly unsafe, and for many of us, socializing via the computer is a safer way to connect with people. The other side of that coin is that as we socialize more, there are people who have found a way to target us and our personal information via the Internet. For the first time in history, people are bullied via the information highway. We then see the threats that were 'out there', come directly into our homes; our safe environment.

Giving back in a personable way can make us seem vulnerable, but shutting ourselves away from others does not diminish the vulnerability. Connecting with our fellow human beings is a positive way to learn, overcome our insecurities and diminish our feelings of disconnect and thoughts of being alone with our problems. Speaking out on issues such as peace is best done when we can see the human factor in it. Seeing people evokes us emotionally, and our thoughts and emotions can connect us and lead us into action. It helps us to understand that we are not alone.

Socializing via the computer diminishes our ability to project positive energy in a powerful way and diminishes our desire for personal contact. Personal contact gives us strength and support and this is a great way to give back to others. Yes, we can give back via the computer but it does not carry the same power as getting out there and doing it in person. The voice of another human being can carry so much compassion and empathy so as to lift another person from their suffering. A gentle touch or hug or assistance to someone can heal so much faster and easier than the written word. We are more likely to support a cause if we can talk with someone who is asking for our support. It is easier to press a delete button on a keyboard when the support is elicited via an email without the human aspect attached. We need human contact. We also need to feel productive in our lives so that we have a sense of accomplishment. Giving back is a great way to feel a sense of accomplishment. Our self esteem and sense of pride is elevated, our mental health is more stable and our overall sense of well being is improved.

One aspect I believe is being missed here is virtue. Living a virtuous life is powerful and permeates our emotions, thoughts and actions. Living virtuously, or as virtuously as possible each and every day, will bring results that will definitely help you find and stay on your true path. Many people try to live the teachings of 'The Secret' but find this is only bringing them limited results. This is because the Virtues of Living are left out of it. But the true path to Enlightenment and manifestation cannot be brought to fruition if you are not virtuous. Dr. Wayne Dyer wrote a book called *Change Your Thoughts, Change Your Life*, outlining the Tao Te Ching's 81 verses of Virtuous Living, based on the teachings of Lao-tzu. These qualities are 2500 years old and are crucial to living your authentic life and becoming more enlightened. All of the verses in this book still pertain to today's society and truly transcends culture, religion and time. In my opinion, it is one of best modern day translations of the Tao.

Now, I'm not saying that you have to live like Mother Teresa or a Monk to be able to live an enlightened existence. You can still live a fulfilling, exciting, adventurous life, but by incorporating these virtues, your life will become more fulfilling, exciting and adventurous. Your life will become richer and your positive energy will become inexhaustible. You can truly give back more of yourself through everything you do. Don't worry about living each good quality 24 hours a day 365 days a year; this will make you paranoid, especially in the beginning. Learn the virtues, incorporate as much as you can each day, and understand that you are an ordinary human being bound to get caught up in everyday life with all that it entails. You are not going to 'hell in a hand basket' if you do not learn all of the virtues. As you learn more and the teachings become ingrained, they will become your way of life. The qualities will play a bigger part of your life than the negative aspects do. You will find yourself giving back without the need for conscious awareness that it is time for you to give back.

For today, and everyday hereafter, be aware and make attempts to give back to your world. We have already taken so much and the evidence is clear: we no longer know our neighbours well, we have an environmental disaster on our hands with global warming, people are no longer shocked by violent behaviour towards our fellow man, more children are ending up in jails due to felony behaviour, and our moral fibre has decayed immensely.

I remember when I was a child; all of our neighbours not only knew each other but were friends. All the neighbourhood kids got together and played with each other. It was safe for us to walk our neighbourhoods at night, at least much safer than it is now. I'm not a Pollyanna and I do realize that danger has always existed, but when something dangerous happened we co-operated with police and the danger was removed. We banned together as a united front against violence and criminal behaviour but sadly that does not happen today. The criminals take over whole cities and the law abiding citizens are held hostage in their communities. This is truly sad. Knowing that positive energy resonates at a higher frequency than negative energy, we do have the power to decrease the negative energy. Like the saying 'Fear knocked on the door, Love opened it, and nothing was there', we can decrease and eliminate negativity and negative actions that come to us by giving back, living virtuously and always facing negativity with positive, loving kindness.

Practice giving back and living virtuously today, tomorrow and every day, and you will see the difference in your life. You have the ability to lift yourself out of suffering and you are able to lift others out of their suffering. We all have this divine energy and it is us who choose what we want to release from our divine essence. Each and every one of us, barre none, has these gifts. If we all choose to use them, we can and will change the world we live in. Remember that you can change the world, and your existence within it.

CHAPTER 9

LIVING YOUR LIFE TO THE FULLEST

What does living your life to the fullest mean? Are we not, by virtue of our existence, living our lives to the fullest? We're here aren't we? Living and breathing, being and doing?

Within all of us is a divine essence or energy in which we were made and that divine essence is our true path of existence as humans; to live, to fulfill, to experience all the wonders, treasures and abilities that the Universe wants us to have. The greatest existence, the most fulfilled that we can be, the most loving, kind and generous spirit we can produce, is truly living your life to the fullest. We are extremely full of all of these things. We choose how to live within our own existence. If we choose to live with negativity, poverty, suspicion, hatred, fear and ignorance, we will create those things in our lives. The others in our lives will help us to reproduce more of that; our relationships, the jobs we get, the money we make, the places we live, will all help us to reproduce that which we think about. But what it all comes down to is your mind, your thoughts, your emotions aligning with your energy to produce all that you have inside you at this very moment.

Don't be discouraged by this because you can, at any moment, change your existence and start to live your life to the fullest. I encourage you to ask yourself this question: In every aspect of my life, am I living to the fullest?

The areas that I am asking you to look at are:

- leisure activities (includes hobbies and downtime activities)

- health (access to health care, exercise, nutrition, mental, emotional)

- work (includes volunteer work)

- relationships (every one of them, including: family, colleagues, friends, animals, environmental and others whom you interact with on a regular basis)

- spirituality and/or religion (includes positive mindset and energy flow)

- education (formal and informal)

- relaxation and/or meditation

- socialization (includes relationships, humour and other interactions)

- money/finances

- housing (shelter)

- giving back (include creativity & inspiration)

In which areas are you strongest? And in which areas do you have challenges? Do you have a good balance of these in your life currently? I don't want to hear the excuses about not having time to have all of these aspects, let alone a balance of them. If you don't currently have all of these aspects in your life, or if they are out of balance on a consistent basis, then something needs to change. You can and do have these characteristics in your life, you may not recognize them, but dollars to donuts you certainly have them and you have the means to access them.

All of these aspects are very important to leading a fulfilled life. Having a balance of these facets are equally important. I do recognize that there are times in our lives when we have to put more of our energy into one or two areas, but these should always end up balancing out. You can actually become addicted to any of these areas and throw your life out of balance, causing you to become maladaptive in your functioning. Most of us have heard the term 'workaholic', this term describes a person with a lack of balance in his or her life. Individuals, who get into addictive relationships, exercise too much, are addicted to money or power, etc. can all become dysfunctional. If more and more of their time and energy is directed towards these aspects of their lives, other areas of their lives become lessened or non-existent.

It does not take money, time or energy to be kinder, or more generous of spirit to others. We just need to adjust our perception of our world. You choose how you react, perceive, and live in this world. You can make better choices and bring about a more positive life for yourself.

If you are in your car driving and your mind, thoughts, and emotions are anxious about getting to your destination, you are likely to hit every stop light, get caught behind slow moving vehicles or questionable drivers and will therefore increase your perception of being late. This only creates more anxiety, anger, and frustration and less time for you. If you take your mind off of your destination and relax, play some good music, and go with the flow of time and traffic, you will find that you will get to your destination on time, if not sooner, in a more relaxed and happier state. Your negative mental and physical effects of stress and anxiety will be greatly reduced. If you are kinder and let in drivers who are trying to merge, you will be more relaxed. It takes no effort on your part; it restores your positive energy and keeps you in better health. What you do while sitting in traffic is your choice, so why not benefit yourself and others by manifesting some positive energy and keeping the road rage at bay?

Living your life to the fullest does not require great wealth, or peak physical conditioning, nor does it require that you do everything for others, neglecting yourself. Living life to the fullest is about balance, treating yourself with love and respect so that you can give love and respect to others, and taking care of yourself so that you can help others. Life doesn't require you to give up the things that you love to do because they may be frowned upon by others. Living your life to the fullest is about creating the best life for you without taking away from others. If you decide that you must have something that another person has and you use manipulation or other negative means to gain that, then you are not living your life to the fullest.

Using and cheating others will bring about negative energy and, in Buddhist terms, negative 'Karma' which is Cause and Effect. The Universe has laws that are in effect at all times. They work perfectly and they can work swiftly. One of the Universal Laws that I think is important for you to remember is the Law of Cause and Effect. This law ensures that there is a consequence or reaction for every action and that it is equal and opposite. So if you think that you are the only one who will know if you have cheated someone, guess again. Ever wonder why bad things are always happening to unscrupulous individuals? They are the first to lament that they just can't catch a break and when they do, they cause something negative to happen soon afterwards. They are manifesting more of what they are putting out – that is negative energy.

Please understand that the act of doing something kind or generous for someone should not come with the proviso that you will get something in return. It should be done with the understanding that you can be a better, kinder and more generous person for yourself and others, leading to a more fulfilled life. That is what you will get in return. This is the Universal Law of Reciprocity. I'm not saying that good things won't happen for you, because they will, and you may manifest all that you desire, but it will not happen when you achieve those desires through unscrupulous or 'tit-for-tat' means, at least not for long.

The Universal Laws, like the Physical Laws, work perfectly all the time. Suffice it to say, that if we work with these perfect laws we will live our lives to the fullest, and more so than we can imagine. I have mentioned the Law of Cause and Effect but I think it is wise to talk a bit about the other Universal Laws so that you can create synergy with them and move your life in accordance with them.

Now we don't question physical laws on a daily basis. When we were getting to know them we did question them, but now we understand a bit about them, and trust that they work perfectly all the time. The Law of Gravity is a great example; in school we learned about the law of gravity. We tested it to see how it worked and then we trusted that it is what it is and it must be that way for the betterment of humankind, and all other living things. We did not however, learn the Universal Laws in school. We did not test them, nor did we learn to understand them. It is now up to us to learn them, test them for ourselves, and trust that they work for the betterment of humankind and all other living things. I am profoundly grateful to have been taught about them by Monks and mentors, and been able to test them for myself and trust that they work for me, as well as for every living thing on this planet.

As my Monk said to me when I first started practicing Buddhism, "Don't just believe what I tell you, try these things and see for yourself." And so I did, with many questions, and I saw for myself that these laws and practices do work and are continuously working. This is why I feel compelled to help others to learn these truths and see for themselves. When you come upon something that is great; a huge sale, a great hair stylist, a trick to help you learn easier, a great resource, someone who has helped you immensely in some way, you spread the word and you become enthusiastic about it and you feel compelled to tell others. I am experiencing the same thing.

I have experienced what others would deem 'miracles' and I guess they are by our human standards, but what I have come to realize is that these are the Universal Laws at work when they are used [properly], and it's absolutely amazing. Why wouldn't I want to let as many people as possible know about them? It serves me no useful value to keep this to myself. I use these laws daily and don't tell people that I am using them at any given time, this we should keep to ourselves. However, learning that they exist, what they are about and how to use them is what should be shared, and this is why I do what I do.

I am not, by any means, a Meta Physicist or Quantum Physicist, nor am I a physicist of any type. But in learning from physicists, as well as about Buddhism, the Universal Energy Source and the Universal Laws and psychology, I have been brought to a place where I have gained a deeper understanding of what can be manifested for our lives and for all living things of which we are all connected.

The **Universal Laws** as I see them have sub-laws, but I am not going to get into all the sub-laws here. Suffice it to say the main laws are highly effective in the way that they work and should be fully understood before moving onto more intricate sub-laws. There are many wise people who explain fully what the sub-laws are all about.

The first Universal Law I will speak about (they are in no particular order) is the **Law of Perpetual Transmutation**. This means that energy, what we and everything in our world is made up of, moves in and out of form.

This means that even a thought moves into an idea then moves into being. This is how all things are made, even us. When we visualize something and then align it with what we desire, the formless begins to take form. Things start to happen and this explains a lot of things that we sometimes just can't put our fingers on, or put it down to coincidence, or déjà vous.

You may be thinking about someone whom you haven't spoken with in a long time and then they call you. Or you think about a certain job you want that just feels right for you and you get hired for it. What you think about, you bring about. This has been tested numerous times throughout history and is used in training Olympic athletes and Astronauts, as well as for many other purposes. We call this **Visualization,** and sports psychologists use it with teams to help them perform better in events. What we don't realize is that we all use this from time to time and then dismiss it as something miraculous or magical when the outcome appears. This isn't the case at all. If we could all understand this and use it for the betterment of ourselves and others, we would all benefit.

Another Universal Law that we work with is the **Law of Vibration** with a sub heading of **Law of Attraction**. Different energy vibrates at different levels, it never rests. We see this in our consciousness as our feelings. It is used with everything that carries energy, which is everything around us. Have you ever heard someone say that they saw the person of their dreams across a crowded bar, their eyes met and there was a huge connection? Love at first sight, or the initial attraction was so overwhelming that they were stuck in this gaze? It happens, and that is the Law of Vibration. This law has connected two people who were resonating at the same energy level. Some call it magnetism, and it works when we are attracting what we need at that moment in our lives.

Your level of vibrational energy will determine what you attract into your life. Another, more negative, example of this is when we hear people say that you look like a 'target'. Security forces all over the world teach people how not to look like a target for criminals. I learned this when taking my community safety training as part of working with high risk populations. We are told what criminals look for in a target and how to avoid this. We are told not to walk with our heads down, to always be aware of our surroundings and to carry our purses or bags in a certain way so as to make it harder for would-be thieves to take advantage of us. This is the way in which your energy is sending out a clear message that you are in fear, and people who want to evoke fear will pick up this energy easily.

We attract what we put out to the world and if we put out fear, low self worth or any negative energy, we will attract this all back to us. It is essential to those who want to change their lives from negative to positive to understand this. And for those who already live in positive energy, they need to understand this so that they can direct their positive energy to those who are suffering.

The **Law of Polarity** speaks about opposites. We have a North and South Pole, things are hot or cold, there is an up and a down, a good and a bad. You can use this in everyday life. If you see that someone is grumpy, rather than get caught up in their negative vibrational energy, you can change it. Give that person a compliment or a smile. It will help them to change their state of mind and their energy. Do something good for someone who is looked upon as a scoundrel or as mean spirited. You have the choice to match their energy or counter it. In the case of negative energy, always try to counter it. This will be better for everyone.

Often times, when a person does something against our morals or mores, we shun that person. We go to a place of condemning them. What we should do is attempt to understand them, why they did what they did and then try to forgive them. We don't have to condone what they did, but in understanding and forgiving them, we stand a better chance of helping them to overcome their own negativity and move to a more positive place. We see this most in criminology. A person commits a horrendous crime against someone else, and the victim or their family forgives the criminal. Our egos would like to go to a place of vengeance and revenge but in forgiving the criminal, many times the criminal goes on to forgive themselves for who they are and what they've done. The criminal then begins to change his or her own life for the better. We would not know good if there was no polar opposite to compare it to.

Another Universal Law is the **Law of Rhythm**. In the universe, and particularly in our world, we see the Law of Rhythm all the time. The tide comes in and then it goes out, the moon holds a particular rhythm with the sun, and there are positive events and thoughts that happen followed by negative events, thoughts, etc which follow them. Everything happens in cycles. We can see this within our own mind. Seasonal Affective Disorder (SAD) comes to mind and is linked to diminished sunlight during the winter months. In the winter, those suffering with SAD feel depressed during times of little sunlight but are fine during the late spring to early autumn when there are more hours of daylight. Astrology works in rhythm, the lunar cycles work this way as well.

If we can recognize and understand that there is a rhythm to everything, we can use the Universal Law of Rhythm to help us. We can stop fighting with the natural rhythm of things and "go with the flow". . Your life will not be all rosy 100 percent of the time, but if you know and accept this as natural, you can then stop fighting against it, which does no good anyway. You can begin to experience life as more positive than negative and effectively and positively deal with the sufferings of life, keeping them to a minimum. Both Deepak Chopra and Ekhart Tolle state that they are happy most all of the time. This does not mean that suffering in some way does not enter into their worlds, it just means that they accept what does come in knowing that they will experience it in a more positive and temporary way; they are in rhythm with the Universe.

I spoke earlier about 'Karma' or **Cause and Effect** and now I will discuss the **Law of Reciprocity.** This law dictates that for every action, there is an equal and opposite reaction, or a consequence for every action, whether the consequence is positive or negative. What you put out there comes back to you. The vibrational energy involved in the action, whether it is negative or positive, will be met equally. Emitting positive energy through your behaviours will come back to you through positive energy.

Practice kindness in every interaction you have. Meet negativity with positive energy. It doesn't cost you anything to practice these things. It will however, benefit you greatly. We have been taught since childhood that we need to think about what we are doing because there are consequences to our actions. This is what this Law all about. We got punished as children for doing something bad or wrong. We learn from our actions and know how to right the wrong next time.

We learn quickly that if we put red clothing in with our whites, there is a good chance we will end up with some pink clothes. We don't make that mistake again. We also learn immediately that if we touch something hot we get burned, and we don't do that consciously again. This law is what a large portion of Behaviour Modification is based on. We teach people to modify their behaviour, by instilling consequences and rewards. If a child does his or her chores for a week they may be rewarded with an allowance. This reward reinforces the child so that he or she will continue to do chores. It is how we learn and grow as human beings. If a child never faces a consequence, that child may never learn how to reciprocate with others and will stand to live an isolated existence from his or her peers.

Another Universal Law that you may be familiar with is the **Law of Relativity.** This law states that everything we perceive is gauged by how it relates to something else. For example, we would not know that we are inside someplace if there was not an outside to relate it to. We know how well we are doing financially based on how others in the same line of work or with the same education are doing. We may think that a person is tall or short, but only because it relates to the overall average height in any given culture. If you come from a family with an overall average height of 5 feet, you may think that you are tall if you are 5'2". But in relation to the overall population, you may still be considered shorter than most.

I hear people all the time, especially in Canada, talking about the weather. We go through a cold, harsh winter and when springtime rolls around and the weather starts to get nice, people say that it's cold. I say that it's warm in relation to the winter we just went through. Our perceptions are guided by this law as well. We perceive things to be easy or difficult based on our past experiences or beliefs about them.

I have difficulties in the area of technology and am a self proclaimed techno-clutz. If a program is 'user friendly' I will somehow manage to make it 'user unfriendly'. This is relative to the amount of education I have in this area and the style in which I learn. If someone goes through something with me 'hands on' and I can do it for myself, then it is easy. If not, then it becomes a nightmare for me.

I am learning to embrace technology and become one with it, but I know where my limitations are and have hired an assistant to help me who is knowledgeable about these things. This way I don't spend the vast majority of my time getting lost in cyberspace and feeling stressed out. I also have someone who I can access to teach me about technology. My perception is that, based on my experience with online technology, I need to be educated about it. When I am educated, technology does not seem so scary.

The last law that I am going to speak about here is the **Law of Gender**. We, as well as every living thing on earth, carry a masculine and feminine energy. To live optimally, we need to have a balance of masculine and feminine energy. This is true for every living thing. This also means that there is a gestation period, or incubating period, for all living things to grow. This is the same for our energy, thoughts and desires to manifest. It's about giving time and space for our ideas, thoughts, feelings and actions to bring about what we want and need.

When a plant grows, it starts from a seed and that seed develops through an incubation period before it grows into a plant. We don't just see a tomato grow the instant we plant its seed. We need to wait for a period of time for the development of the tomato. Our spiritual energy is like a seed. We plant the idea and the Universe moves that idea, thought, or energy into form. Sometimes we can manifest what we need quickly and other times we need to wait for the ideas to become evident. The Law of Gender will always make visible what we are in terms of our thoughts, feelings and actions, or intentions. When the time is right, what you desire will manifest. There is a right time for everything.

Our egos tend to claim that this does not happen, or that it is not happening when we want it to, in the way that you want it to, so it must not work. Remember that this is just the ego speaking. We should not ever try to control how something comes into our lives when it needs to happen. You can only put out to the Universe what you would like and it will take care of the rest. Just know that it will.

How many times have you been so focused that you literally brought what you were thinking into fruition? For example, you are so focused on moving and a dream job at your company becomes open in the very area you wish to move to. You suddenly are hired for this job. I was so focused on buying my parents house from them and they were waiting for me to do so, I only had one concern - that was to have enough of a down payment so that my mortgage payments would be affordable. Well a week or so after having this conversation with my mom about my concern and both of us being so focused on this deal, I won a lottery and gave my mother the winning ticket as the down payment for the house. I didn't have to concern myself with the mortgage payments because the ticket was worth $125,000.00.

This is not a fluke; I can recall many instances when this sort of thing has happened. Sometimes the manifestations come into play instantly and other times I must wait. But I am patient and don't allow my ego to get in the way of this gestation period because I know that it will happen when the time is right for it to happen. And I don't try to control how it will come to me because the Universe has its own ways of bringing about what you need and it may

be in a way that you could never have imagined. I have learned to view life as a kind of treasure hunt. I know that magnificent things are happening; I just have to keep my eyes open and look for the opportunities. I have to let it all unfold exactly as it's meant to. Life is very exciting to me now, whereas it was looking gloomy and bleak for a long time. It wasn't until I started becoming educated about and started using the Universal Laws and our mind's own capabilities that my life started to change in amazing ways, so profoundly and so deeply.

Now I know about different facets of the Universal Laws regarding what is the main law and what is the sub law. In my research and inquiries, these laws are the most stable of the many universal laws that we work with in our lives. We are still, and will continue to find out more about these laws, as well as, discovering more laws and sub laws. Because of their benefit to all living things, we should open our minds and our lives to them. They are always going to work the way that they should, and they will work perfectly all of the time. It is us that refuse to let ourselves work in alignment with them. I've stated many times before, sometimes we just need to get out of our own way!

It is my belief that if you use the strategies in this chapter to inform yourself and implement these Universal Laws, you will be able to live a truly fulfilled life. You must take action on your path in life. No one else walks your life path and so no one is going to do the necessary work for you, you need to do it for yourself. There may be people in your life who know what is best for you, but you are the only one who truly knows what is right for you, based on your unique perceptions, spirit and beliefs.

CHAPTER 10

SYNOPSIS

I hope after reading this book, you have developed a clearer understanding of some of the strategies you can use overcome negative or problematic behaviours. I also hope you have learned how your energy works and how you can use it to connect you to the Universal Energy Source to elevate your spirituality to higher levels. In turn, you are gaining the ability to manifest all that you visualize to be your desired life.

Every human being, except for the 0.01 percent of cells that make us unique, is the same when it comes down to our structure and ingredients. We are all connected through molecules, protons, energy and cells that die off and then rejuvenate at an incredible speed. According to Deepak Chopra, a medical doctor, our entire set of body cells rejuvenates in one year.

When we are ridding ourselves of every type of cell in our bodies, we are sending them out into the world to mingle with everyone else's cells. We inhale and exhale and take a part of someone else with us at the same time we are getting rid of ourselves. How can we not be interconnected? It is our culture, environment, belief systems and perceptions that set us so seemingly far apart. What a shame that we can't just recognize our differences and understand that, as divine human beings, we are absolutely allowed to be dissimilar. Our differences should not have to lead to war, abuse or discrimination.

No human being should be seen as less than that. Who are we to pass that judgement? Yes, we do have laws that help maintain a sense of order, but we see those laws exploited every day all over the globe. Rules help to define where we come from, what our mores are, and what our cultural differences are. In my opinion, rules should be kept simple, straight forward, and be set up to help us become better people. I think that the old world texts pretty much covered all we need to be better people, with morals and values woven in. It seems today that there is a substantial amount of moral decay.

The Universe has always provided us with what we need to, not only survive, but thrive. I am excited about the Universal shift of consciousness occurring in the world and I am happy to be one of those agents of change. Whether I help two people or two million people, I am part of the change process. And you can be as well. The strategies in this book will work for you if you use them. You owe it to yourself, as well as all the rest of us, to try.

Your divine essence is a guiding light in your life, even if you don't see it at the moment. If you still your thoughts and listen to your energy, your subconscious and your spirit will guide you and provide for you all the elements you need to live an extraordinary life beyond your dreams. Even if this book provides you with the means to better communicate with your loved ones, or boosts your self-esteem, I am so grateful for that because I know that you deserve it.

When you understand the psychology of the human mind, you come to realize that there are human needs that are Universal and that we don't have to be from the same culture, race, ethnicity or environment to embrace them. They are inside every human being and they transcend any other factors that we bring with us into this human existence. They make up our Spiritual source.

I have no thoughts about 'competing' with any other existing agents of change. I come from a place of abundance, and I believe that we all will be provided with everything we desire. I didn't write this book to make a lot of money, or write this book with the perception that there are plenty of books on the market today that help people to change their lives. I simply looked inside myself and was guided. I did not even consciously choose the subjects to write about, or determine what context to put them into. I also did not need to do a lot of research. This book was born out of the experiences I have, the path that is my calling and the knowledge I have attained throughout the years; not only with my education, but, more importantly, through the guidance of the Universal Source.

In listening to that guiding source, all of the resources I need have been provided and all the people that have helped me along my path have emerged. With each step, another door opens, and in having trust in the Universe to not use my ego and second guess each decision, I have had my path laid out for me. I remember back in the day when I lived in my ego and did not know of this guiding energy. I didn't realize what my life was like and why it wasn't turning out the way I had hoped. I have since learned why that was.

It was a very dark period of my life and I literally didn't think I could withstand anymore. My spiritual energy was strong but my ego was stronger and I just knew that I could control my world. Now that I look back to that time, I realize how naive I was to ever think that I had control. My ego had control and I was merely a pawn in its game. Fortunately for me, my Spiritual energy was what I always wanted to listen to but I just didn't know how to hear it. I was practically screaming for something more when I timidly stood outside of the door to a Buddhist Temple, shaking and scared that I would be embarking on more than I could handle at that point. It turned out to be one of the best decisions I've ever made in my life.

Work Cited

Egan, G (1994). *The Skilled Helper*. Belmont, CA: Wadsworth Inc.

Gunaratana, H (1992). *Mindfulness in Plain English*. Boston, MA: Wisdom Publications.

Prochaska J.O, Norcross J.C, & Diclemente C.C (1994). *Changing For Good*. New York, NY: William Morrow and Company, Inc.